Divorced Parents
and Their Children

Dorothy W. Cantor, Psy.D. received her doctorate from the Graduate School of Applied and Professional Psychology, Rutgers University, where she now serves as a Visiting Assistant Professor, and Director of Continuing Education. She has written and lectured extensively on the subjects of the effects of divorce on children and appropriate intervention techniques for those children and their parents. Dr. Cantor is in private clinical practice in Westfield, New Jersey.

Ellen A. Drake, Psy.D., received her doctorate from the Graduate School of Applied and Professional Psychology, Rutgers University. Dr. Drake is a candidate for post-doctoral certification in psychoanalysis and psychotherapy at New York University. She is listed in *Who's Who of American Women*. She is the author of numerous articles published in professional journals and has lectured widely on the topic of divorce. Dr. Drake is in private clinical practice in Kendall Park, New Jersey.

Divorced Parents and Their Children

A Guide for Mental Health Professionals

Dorothy W. Cantor, Psy.D.
Ellen A. Drake, Psy.D.

Foreword by Richard A. Gardner, M.D.

SPRINGER PUBLISHING COMPANY
New York

To Bernard Wolf,
who would be pleased with
the hard cover
and
To Cliff with love

Springer Publishing Company, Inc.
200 Park Avenue South
New York, New York 10003

84 85 86 87 88 / 10 9 8 7 6 5 4 3 2

Library of Congress Cataloging in Publication Data

Cantor, Dorothy W.
  Divorced parents and their children.
  Bibliography: p. Includes index.
  1. Divorced parents—Mental health. 2. Children of divorced parents—Mental health. I. Drake, Ellen A. II. Title. [DNLM: 1. Divorce. 2. Parent-child relations. 3. Child psychology. WS 105.5.A8 C229d]
RJ507.D59C36 1983   362.8'286   83-457
ISBN 0-8261-3560-9

Printed in the United States of America

Contents

Foreword

Divorce conflict, in many ways, can reasonably be viewed as a kind of war. Both sides marshall their forces and attempt to enlist the aid of anyone who might be of potential value in helping the belligerent win. In traditional wars, there is generally a lower age limit for the recruits, but this is not the case in the kind of war called divorce. If a child can be useful in serving the cause of the warring parents, his services are likely to be enlisted. In traditional warfare, borders are carefully guarded to prevent the infiltration of spies (who might convey important information back to the enemy) and saboteurs (who might destroy installations and other sites vital to the war effort). In divorce war, just the opposite is the case. The potential spies and saboteurs (the children) are literally welcomed with open arms into enemy territory. Such opportunities are rarely neglected, thereby intensifying the conflict.

As is true of all wars, the psychological trauma that the belligerent suffer is often formidable. Although divorce per se does not necessarily cause parents and children to suffer psychological disturbances, the situation certainly increases the risk for the development of such disorders. There are certainly divorces in which the parents handle themselves in a relatively civilized manner—so much so that neither they nor their children experience significant negative reactions. In fact, in some cases the divorce proves to be a psychologically beneficial experience in that it reduces the exposure of all family members to the detrimental situation. Unfortunately, such "civilized" divorces are in the minority. The more usual situation is one in which there is an ongoing conflict to which the children are usually exposed if not actively embroiled. And, the longer the conflict, the greater the likelihood both parents and children will suffer psychological disturbance. In fact, when such conflicts are protracted (especially as the result of litigation), the development of psychopathological reactions by both parents and children could reasonably be considered inevitable.

In this book the authors provide mental health professionals with a wealth of information designed to instruct and assist them in helping their clients prevent and deal with some of the most common problems that confront divorced parents and their children. The emphasis throughout is on helping parents diminish the risk of the development of psychopathology in their children. Their advice is ever practical and clearly presented.

A wide range of issues with which divorced parents are faced are dealt with: How, who, when, and what to tell the children; avoiding the use of children as spies and weapons; parenting optimally in the single-parent household (both for the custodial and the noncustodial parent); the visitation experience; preventing children's negative reactions to dating and sleep-over friends; and dealing with the special problems of the stepfamily. Throughout there are frequent references to pertinent articles in the literature. In fact, the bibliography and the appendix of recommended readings could serve well as an up-to-date review of the literature on this timely subject.

It is particularly gratifying to note the authors' deep appreciation of the limitations of *individual* treatment for divorced parents and their children. Although they recognize its role in the treatment of the intrapsychic problems with which such people may suffer, they emphasize that the interpersonal problems are the ones that generally require particular attention in divorced families. They recognize fully the value of family and/or group therapy, in that these treatment modalities may provide the best hope for alleviation of the interpersonal problems related to the divorce conflict. Therapists today are becoming increasingly appreciative of the fact that divorce status should not preclude joint counseling. Therapists are increasingly learning (often through bitter experience) that treating warring ex-spouses separately (most often by separate therapists) is likely to be a futile endeavor with regard to the alleviation of the divorce conflict. So important is this point that I would say that one of the most important indications for *family therapy* is the treatment of *divorced parents* and their children. There is no paradox here. Divorced people are still psychologically part of a family—their legal status not withstanding.

The importance of bringing step-parents into such family sessions as well is emphasized by the authors. My experience has been that such step-parental involvement can add a valuable contribution to the treatment of the divorced family, and the failure to include such persons (initial reservations notwithstanding) can retard immeasurably the progress of such therapy. The authors are to be especially commended for their Post-Divorce Parenting Program (for *both* parents) which provides educational and therapeutic experiences for divorced parents. The program is particularly geared to helping such parents deal with and prevent psychological disturbances in their children.

The book's discussions of custody conflicts and custody litigation are illuminating. Of all the problems in the divorce situation that are likely to produce psychopathology in both parents and children, there is no question that protracted custody litigation can cause the greatest degree of damage. There is little question that attorneys (their avowels of serving the best interests of the children notwithstanding) contribute significantly to the polarization of the parents that is the primary cause of such psychopathology. The authors strongly discourage mental health professionals from serving as advocates in such litigation and wisely encourage their participating, if at all possible, as impartial experts. This warning cannot be sounded loudly enough. Mental health professionals who serve as advocates are likely to do more harm than good. When each side brings up its parade of "hired guns," each of whom has only seen one parent, the professional testimonies become meaningless. Such spectacles (and they occur every day) are a disgrace to mental health professionals and are a disservice to the legal profession as well. But even worse, they prolong the tensions and anxieties of the parents, add to the expense of the litigation, contribute thereby to the intensification of the psychopathology inevitably attendant to such litigation.

In conclusion, I highly recommend the book to mental health professionals involved in counseling and treating divorced parents and their children. Implementation of this book's advice can prove useful in both preventing and treating the wide variety of psychological disorders so commonly seen in divorced parents and their children.

Richard A. Gardner, M.D.
Associate Clinical Professor
of Child Psychiatry
Columbia University, College
of Physicians and Surgeons

Preface

This book was written to provide a single source of information for mental health professionals who come into contact with divorced parents to assist the professionals in working with the parents and their children. As the incidence of divorce steadily rises, mental health professionals who work in schools, community mental health centers, and private practice settings are seeing an increasing number of divorced individuals. These professionals have been trained as counselors or therapists, but are often not cognizant of the issues involved in divorce for children and their parents or in how to integrate their knowledge about divorce-related issues into their practices.

The authors have not espoused a single therapeutic modality nor a single theoretical model. We have assumed that the mental health professionals who read this book will adapt the information to their own therapeutic orientation and style.

The authors recognize that there traditionally have been differences between the role of the mother and the father in the family. Where these differences impact on divorce-related issues, such as custody and visitation, they are discussed. Otherwise, the assumption is made that principles of good parenting apply equally to parents of both sexes.

Although this book is addressed to mental health professionals, it may be useful to members of the legal profession as well. Lawyers and judges are involved in every case of divorce and an expansion of their knowledge regarding the impact of divorce on children can help influence the way in which they handle adversarial divorce proceedings when children are involved.

We wish to thank Richard A. Gardner, M.D., for his encouragement and his contribution of the Foreword, Barbara Watkins for her careful editorial attention to our work, and our families for their patience and support as we worked on this project.

Dorothy W. Cantor, Psy.D.
Ellen A. Drake, Psy.D.

Chapter 1

The Effects of Divorce on Children

It is important that the mental health professional who works with divorced parents be aware of the effects divorce has on children. Knowing what is expected helps the professional to distinguish between normal and pathological responses to the separation/divorce and helps evaluate behaviors upon which interventions can be based. An analogy can be made to understanding a person grieving the death of a loved one. The professional who anticipates a normal grief period that includes denial, anger, and depression will react differently from one who does not expect such responses. Equipped with such knowledge about children of divorce, the professional can better evaluate the problem, assess the responses, help parents to help their children, and know when and how to intervene.

Statistics on Divorce

The most recent statistical information can be found in the *Population Bulletin* of October 1977 entitled "Marrying, Divorce and Living Together in the U.S. Today" (Glick & Norton, 1979), and in the summer 1979 Census Bureau Report: *Divorce, Child Custody and Child Support* (Bureau of the Census, 1979).

The divorce rate in the United States has far exceeded that of any other country. Between 1965 and 1976, the annual divorce rate doubled from 2.5% to 5% per 1,000 population. For Americans, divorce court is second only to traffic court as a source of exposure to the judicial system. Three out of four divorces occur in families with children. The average length of marriage is 6¾ years and the median length of marriage is 5 years.

Each year, over a million children under the age of 18 are involved in marital breakups. In 1978, 4.5 million children lived with a divorced parent. The proportion of children under 18 living only with their mothers has doubled since 1960, from 8% to 16%. The proportion of children of divorce who live with only their fathers is 1.6%. The statistics show that 33% of children under 18 do not live with their families of origin and, for black children, the percentage is 45%. It is estimated that as many as 45% of all children born in 1977 are likely to live for at least several months as members of a one-parent family (Bureau of the Census, 1979).

For mental health professionals, the percentage of their caseloads devoted to divorced parents and their children will vary depending on the setting of their practice. The authors have found in their private practice settings that about one-third of the adults referred are either divorced or considering divorce, while one-third to one-half of children referred are children of divorce. The percentage of children is comparable in an out-patient mental health center or among those children referred to a school child study team. Gross, Dibbell, and Petti (1977) reported that in a school system of 15,000 students, one-third of the referrals to the child study team were children of divorce. A study at the University of Rochester (Felner, Stolberg, & Cowen, 1975) found that 20% of children referred to a clinic had a history of parental separation through either divorce or death. Significantly more aggressive and acting-out problems were found with this population. Teachers report that at least one-quarter of the children in their classrooms have experienced parental divorce. In some communities, we have seen classes where more than half of the children are in that category.

Changes in Family Structure
Resulting from Divorce

Let us consider what happens within a family when a divorce occurs. Before divorce, when the family is functioning well, there is positive interaction within the family between the parents and between each parent and the children. After divorce, when one parent has custody, the other parent's energies are diverted outside the family. One parent is unavailable to the family and the other parent feels obligated to bear the majority of the responsibility of parenting.

In some families, there is a total breakdown in communication between the parents. When that occurs, the children are the source of communication between them. For example, the mother says to the child: "I'm angry with your father because he always gets here late to pick you up," and the child proceeds to tell the father that the mother is angry at him.

Frequently, rather than a total breakdown in communication, there is an outbreak of hostility between the parents. Then, the child is isolated from both parents. It is these family situations, in which there is a total breakdown in communications between parents or an outbreak of hostility between them, that place a heavy burden on the children and are therefore most destructive to them.

What children need when their parents divorce is a situation in which, despite the fact that the husband-wife relationship between the parents no longer exists, the parent-parent relationship does and they continue to communicate regarding their children. The children have lost the superstructure of the family, but they have maintained a relationship with each of their parents. The least possible change in the children's lives has occurred, allowing the stress upon the children to be kept to a minimum.

Some children are able to insist on the healthier pattern by their own behavior. They let their parents know that they need attention from both of them. They may become whiny or demanding. Those children are better off than other children who keep their needs to themselves and become quiet and withdrawn. The children who "act up" may succeed in getting their parents' attention, although negative attention. The quiet child is more likely to be left unattended.

There are a multitude of ways in which children manage to engage their parents' attention around the time of separation. A 5-year-old reverts to bed-wetting; a 9-year-old refuses to go to school; a 14-year-old begins shoplifting. Siblings seem to fight more around their parents. Children who used to be cooperative become stubbornly recalcitrant. All of these behaviors distract the parents from their internal stresses and focus them on the children. However, for the children, these are destructive means of achieving the goal. Mental health professionals can help parents to focus on the children in a manner which is constructive to all those involved.

Studies of Effects of Divorce on Children

Occasional articles about the effects of divorce on children can be found in the literature since the 1930s. More frequent articles are found since the mid-1960s. The increase in interest and research on the topic of children of divorce has paralleled the increased number of children affected. Wallerstein and Kelly began a longitudinal study in California in 1971, and more definitive information about the impact of divorce on children is coming out of their research than previously had been known. Also in 1970, Richard Gardner published *The Boys and Girls Book about Divorce*, that was one of the earliest efforts to reach the children. In 1977, a special issue of the *Journal of Clinical Child Psychology* listed 74 fiction and 8 nonfiction books for children and adolescents. *The Journal of Divorce*, an interdisciplinary journal, began publication in 1977, and many of the articles in the first volume concerned children of divorce. Since 1979, there has been a spate of books for professionals and lay people dealing with the effects of divorce on children and with custody arrangements. (See Appendix B).

Children of divorce can be perceived as an at-risk population. The difficulty with interpreting the available research regarding these children is that the sample size used in the studies tends to be quite small, the use of control groups is rare, other variables are not controlled, and the criteria for diagnosis is not clearly defined across studies. One large study of the records of 400 children reported that children of divorce were referred for outpatient psychiatric evaluation at nearly twice the rate of the general population (Kalter, 1977). Children of divorce had a higher rate of occurrence of antisocial delinquent behavior and of overt aggression toward their parents than did referred children from intact homes. Kalter recommended that future studies control for the age and sex of child patients in order to better understand the special difficulties faced by children of divorce.

Effects of Divorce at Different Developmental Stages

There is no single outcome that can be identified as the inevitable effect of divorce on children. Researchers have noticed patterns that vary from age to age, depending on the developmental tasks and the relative importance of the family constellation at that age. However, as there are multiple variables involved in children's postdivorce adjustment, the interaction of these variables produces unique individual responses within the typical patterns.

Kurdek and Siesky (1980) found age to be the most powerful variable in children's postdivorce adjustment. As children get older, they perceive events as under their control and their level of interpersonal knowledge increases. As a result, they see themselves less as hapless targets and better understand their parents' decision to divorce as being apart from them and their behavior. However, the results of a recent study indicate that two years after the divorce, while children's understanding of the divorce showed few areas of concern, their feelings about the divorce tended to be negative (Kurdek, Blisk, & Siesky, 1981).

Preschool Children

According to Glick (1979), the divorce rate is relatively low in families with preschool children. Only 4.6% of children under age 6, compared with 8.2% of children ages 6 to 17, live with a divorced parent. It may be that having preschool children makes parents somewhat less inclined to divorce.

Wallerstein and Kelly (1975) studied the responses of 34 preschool children at the time of initial separation and one year later. In the youngest group, ages 2½ to 3¼, the children had few ways of relieving their suffering. McDermott (1968) had previously observed that nursery school children react to divorce with an impairment of the capacity to master anxiety and depression through play, one of the ways young children typically employ. All of the children in the preschool group responded to separation with observable, significant behaviorial changes, including acute regressions in toilet training, increased irritability, whining and crying, increased separation anxiety, cognitive confusion, return to transitional objects, and increased autoerotic activities. Symptoms were temporary if continuity of physical and loving care was restored. The most enduring symptoms were pervasive neediness, expressed in a too-quick reaching out to strange adults. The case of Judith, age 13, is an example. Her parents separated when the patient was age 3. Judith, ten years later, continued to demonstrate symptoms of neediness, reaching out quickly to her mother's boyfriends, calling each of them "Daddy" the first time they came to the home.

The middle preschool group, ages 3 ¾ to 4 ¾, were less likely to regress, but irritability, whininess, tearfulness, and aggressiveness increased. These children seemed bewildered at the loss of a parent. Their view of the dependability and predictability of relationships was threatened.

The oldest preschool groups, ages 5 and 6, experienced heightened anxiety and aggression at the time of parental separation, manifested by restlessness, moodiness, and temper tantrums. Children at this age were, unlike younger children, able to verbally express their sadness, their longing for the absent parent, and the wish to restore the family. One mother, on the advice of her attorney, did not allow her estranged husband to see their son. The mother reported when seen in therapy one year after the separation, that the son continued to ask about the father and, at least once a day, questioned when he would see his Dad. The teacher reported to the mother that the boy appeared to be "an unhappy child." Of Wallerstein and Kelly's total preschool sample, 44% were found to be in a significantly deteriorated psychological condition one year later.

Hodges, Wechsler, and Ballantine (1979) challenged the findings of Wallerstein and Kelly's study. Hodges et al. did a study comparing 26 preschool children from divorced homes with 26 children from intact homes. They found relatively few significant differences between the groups. The factors that did predict negative adjustment for the children of divorce were: limited financial resources, relative young age of parents, and geographic mobility. These factors were not significant for children in intact homes. The authors concluded that the effect of stress on young children may be cumulative and that divorce *per se* does not produce significant harm. On the basis of their findings, they hypothesized that a single traumatic event in early childhood of parents separating may be less important than the quality of life and number of life stresses provided by daily living.

School-Age Children

For the school-age child, divorce is likely to interfere with the freedom to focus attention outside of the family on school, and the result is frequently poor school performance. A study by Felner et al. (1975) confirmed the hypothesis that crisis events such as parental death or separation/divorce exact a toll in early school adjustment. Children of divorced parents were found to have elevated acting-out and aggressive referral patterns. (Note: The researchers did not account for the age of the children at the time of the separation.) For latency children, the different roles they had played in the family and the nature of the continuing relationship to the parents, greatly affected the reaction to the separation (Tessman, 1978a).

Wallerstein and Kelly separated their groups into early latency (7- and 8-year-olds) and later latency (9- to 11-year-olds). The 7- and 8-year-olds reacted with sadness and grief, very much like the mourning process associated with death. Children expressed feelings of deprivation and diffuse fears. They felt as if there was no safe refuge. Reconciliation fantasies were common. Most of these feelings abated within a year and were replaced with resignation. However, 23% of the children in this age group were worse a year after the separation (Kelly & Wallerstein, 1976).

The 9-to 11-year-olds (Wallerstein & Kelly, 1976) showed very little regression. They perceived the realities of the family disruption with clarity. Feelings of shame emerged specifically with this age group, but the one feeling that distinguished this group from all younger children was their intense anger, directed frequently at the parent perceived as having caused the divorce. Children in this group experienced a shaken sense of identity and a sense of loneliness. Somatic symptoms appeared in this age group. After a year, in half of the children, the turbulent responses were muted, but one-third of these children still retained angry feelings toward the absent parent. The other half of the group gave evidence of consolidation into conflicted, depressed behavior patterns. An example of the angry feelings was seen in an 11-year-old patient who had learned some Transactional Analysis vocabulary. He spoke in therapy about "saving brown stamps" (i.e., holding in his anger) and, with increasing frequency as the separation became imminent, became aggressive toward his father.

Adolescents

For the adolescent, the developmental tasks of defining identity and adjusting to sexual maturation may be accelerated by the parents' divorce. Adolescents need a stable base to which they can return in the process of gradual emancipation from the parents (Wallerstein & Kelly, 1980). Adolescents in a divorced family, without such a base, feel hurried to complete the developmental process. Divorce weakens external controls and discipline for adolescents. In addition, they are more aware than the youngsters in intact families of their parents as sexual objects (Wallerstein & Kelly, 1974) and, for some, this precipitates premature heterosexual relationships (Hetherington, 1972). When divorcing parents revert to adolescent behaviors, the adolescent children are thrust into a competitive position and, at the same time, lack a mature role model. Wallerstein and Kelly (1974) found that loyalty conflicts aroused feelings of anger, depression and guilt which abated after a year. Withdrawal and distancing were used defensively to protect from the parental crisis. Tessman (1978a) found these behaviors particularly among older adolescents, whose disengagement protected them from disrupting their own development. A study by Reinhard (1977) reported that adolescents were not adversely affected in peer relations or school activities, suggesting that they were able to separate family life from the world outside.

Sorosky (1977) suggested that the experience of parental divorce can create psychological vulnerabilities for adolescents, such as: "(1) a fear of abandonment, rejection or loss of love, (2) an interference with the resolution of the typical adolescent conflicts, and (3) an intense fear of personal marital failure" (p.134). Adam, Lohrenz, and Harper (1973) studied the effect of parental loss on suicidal ideation in adolescents. The results supported the hypothesis that unresolved object loss in childhood may lead to an inability to sustain object losses later in life, with possible subsequent depressive reactions and suicidal behavior.

Most adolescents referred for treatment came in six months to two-and-a-half years subsequent to the divorce (Tessman, 1978b). The referral problems included school problems, overt depression, running away, and increased acting-out behaviors.

Other Variables

Children's divorce adjustment seems related to environmental change and to the patterns of familial reorganization (Kurdek, 1981). Some of the variables that affect adjustment are: the ongoing relationship between the parents, the parents' mental health, changes in lifestyle, the sex of the child, the sex of the custodial parent, and the competencies of the child.

The Ongoing Relationship between the Parents

Just as the relationship between married spouses has a critical effect on the climate of the household and the atmosphere in which the children develop, the ongoing relationship between divorced spouses also has impact on the children. A cooperative, mutually supportive relationship between the divorced spouses reduces the crisis-potentiating stress (Ahrons, 1981). Unfortunately, such a spirit of mutual cooperation around parenting appears to be the exception, rather than the rule. Ahrons (1981) interviewed 54 pairs of divorced spouses and discovered that 50% of the sample perceived their relationship to be conflictual at least some of the time. She noted that the figures are probably higher because the most conflictual and destructive divorces might not have been sampled because of the criteria for inclusion in the study: Fathers had to see children at least once in two months, reside in the community, and volunteer to participate.

Frequently, there remains a great deal of unresolved hostility between divorced spouses. Although many indicate "feeling nothing" for their former mates, when the issue is explored in therapy, they discover some positive but many negative feelings. Clients are often surprised at the interpretation that their anger serves, as would positive feelings, to keep them connected to the former spouse. Unresolved angry feelings create a tense atmosphere in which interparent communication is either absent or volatile. Either creates an uneasy environment for the children.

If parents can come to realize that it is acceptable (and preferable for the children) to feel positively toward a former spouse and that such emotions are not pathological, then they can become more cooperative and supportive of each other in the parenting role. A custodial parent, who still has the other parent for support, is less likely to draw the children into the decision-making process and is more likely to assert appropriate parental authority.

Impact on Children of Parents' Mental Health

Although there is little empirical evidence on the issue, it is evident that the emotional well-being of the parents affects children. The anxiety, fear, anger, guilt, or the myriad of other emotions, particularly of the custodial parent, seldom escape detection by the child, and, the children may "resonate" similar feelings. For example, a depressed parent may create an atmosphere which depresses the child although the ways in which children express the feelings may differ. A depressed parent may use alcohol to try to suppress the discomfort of these feelings whereas the child resonating the depression may act out in school or withdraw from peer relationships.

Similarly, a parent who is fearful may find the child has nightmares. An anxious parent may create a situation in which the child experiences eating difficulties, sleeping problems, school problems, peer problems, and so forth. It would be unusual for a child not to respond in any way to a parent, especially to the one with whom he or she lives.

A current study (Worell, 1981) is testing the hypothesis that some of the psychological disruption observed in children of divorce is related to the quality of the custodial mother's adjustment. Maternal stress is predicted to foster negative and coercive childrearing practices, which, in turn, produce disrupted behavioral and developmental progress in the children.

Changes in Lifestyle

Children watch the transition of their separated parents. There may be changes in weight, hairstyles, or clothes. There may be new friends and changes in choice of music or entertainment. There may be a change in living quarters. At times, there may be less availability of their parents and multiple caretakers may be the norm. Children tend to fear rapid or sudden changes in their parents. They often do not understand the changes. They experience a sense of instability and a tense anticipation of what other changes may be forthcoming.

For many divorced families, there are increased financial pressures that act as an additional stressor on parents and children. Single mothers, who have not previously been employed, find themselves reentering the job market in order to supplement alimony and child support, or to entirely support the family. The result is a diminished amount of time and energy available to the children. Custodial fathers have reported the same stress of reduced financial comfort and increased pressures to manage the multiple tasks of job and household (Keshet & Rosenthal, 1978). For the children, there may be a reduction in the money available for nonnecessities, gifts, and social activities. Each change in lifestyle is an additional stressor to which the children have to adjust.

Sex of the Child

Hetherington (1979) reported that boys seem to be more vulnerable to the adverse effects of divorce than girls and may continue to show developmental deviations as they mature. One hypothesis as to cause is that boys receive less positive reinforcement for compliance than do girls, causing them to rely on negative behavior as a source of attention (Hetherington, Cox, & Cox, 1977). When interacting with sons, divorced parents communicated less, were less consistent, and used more negative sanctions than with their daughters. Wallerstein and Kelly (1980) also found a widening gap between the reactions of boys and girls a year after the divorce. The boys were more depressed, more intensely preoccupied with the divorce, longed for their fathers more, and felt more rejected by their fathers. However, after five years, sex did not appear to be a factor in postdivorce adjustment.

In a recent study, Weingarten and Kulka (1979) replicated national survey data from 1957 and found that adult males who had experienced divorce as children have more difficulty handling problems as adults and have less interest in parenting than adult males who had not experienced divorce as children. By contrast, adult women who had been children of divorce were overly interested in parenting.

Sex of the Custodial Parent

Custodial mothers have been observed to become more restrictive and controlling than their counterparts in intact families. Custodial mothers exhibit more negative behavior such as negative commands, negative sanctions, and opposition to requests towards their sons than towards their daughters (Hetherington et al. 1977).

There are several factors that may contribute to the poorer quality of relationships between mothers and sons than mothers and daughters. The son may be identified as being or looking "like the father" with negative feelings displaced onto him. The Oedipal implications of the mother-son relationship may lead to behaviors on the mother's part unconsciously designed to distance the child. Or, sex-role stereotypes may lead the mother to encourage repression of emotion and acting out by the son. Custodial fathers of daughters can be expected to have similar difficulties around issues of identification, Oedipal conflict, and sex-role stereotyping.

The child with a custodial parent of the same sex has a person present with whom to identify. However, these children frequently experience disruptions in interactions with peers of the opposite sex (Hetherington, 1972). Conversely, the child with an opposite sex custodial parent does not have a constantly present role model and has to identify with a less available individual—the noncustodial parent, or with a step-parent or other surrogate figure.

The Competencies of the Child

The predivorce adjustment of a child is a major factor in postdivorce adjustment. The child who approaches the stressful event with good coping skills is at an advantage. The child who is able to share feelings about the divorce with peers, particularly those who have undergone the same experience, seem to have an easier time adjusting (Cantor, 1977; Kurdek et al. 1981). Also, children who are able to understand that their behaviors or feelings were not the cause of the parents' separation, but that the relationship between the parents was the problem, can better adjust to the divorce (Kurdek, et al. 1981).

Hetherington (1979) has suggested that children's temperament may affect divorce adjustment. "Easy" children adapt well to environmental change. They have positive moods, approach new stimuli readily and react to new situations with low intensity. Such children would be expected to react less negatively to the stress of divorce than would "difficult" children who react poorly to environmental change, have negative moods, approach new stimuli warily and react to new situations with high intensity.

Mitigating Factors

For most children, the distress following parental separation is unlikely to be permanent. Much like mourning upon the death of a loved one, the grief following divorce must run its course. It must follow stages similar to the grief stages of denial, anger, depression, and acceptance. Research indicates that after a year, most symptoms will have abated. Children gradually develop a new level of equilibrium, while maintaining strong loyalty to the predivorce family structure and regarding divorce as painful (Kurdek et al., 1981). Thus, they would choose to have never had the divorce happen, but they are able to go on with their lives and cope with the tasks before them.

Several factors can ease the distress of the first year and increase the likelihood of healthy adjustment. Jacobson (1978a) reported on a study of 30 families, involving 51 children. She concluded that the amount of time not spent with the noncustodial parent is a significant factor in children's postdivorce adjustment. She hypothesized that a child who experiences a high degree of separation from a parent suffers object loss. In her sample, the more time lost from the non-custodial parent, the higher the maladjustment of the child in the 12 months following separation. Therefore, the continuity of the relationship with the noncustodial parent can reduce the stress of the immediate postdivorce period.

The intensity of children's reactions to the divorce is affected by the parents' ability to meet their children's needs for sustained caring during the postdivorce period. Therefore, it is of particular importance that divorcing parents be helped to refocus on their parenting roles. Good parenting skills by both custodial and noncustodial parents are a crucial factor in the postdivorce life of a child and will very much decrease the likelihood of the development of psychopathology.

If parenting is a difficult task for the married parent who is ill-prepared for the task, it is even more so for the divorced parent because of the special problems of parenting created by divorce. Consequently, one of the first tasks of the mental health professional who comes in contact with divorcing parents is to help them keep in mind their parenting responsibilities and then help provide them with the needed skills or resources to be good parents.

Tessman (1978a) posed the question: "What factors or patterns appear to be debilitating rather than enriching to the growth of the child of the divorce?" She then responded:

> a. If he is neglected during the period prior to, during, and after the loss, i.e., if the loss of one parent is compounded by the loss of sustained caring by the remaining parent or other significant adults.
> b. If he is not allowed grief or longing for the absent parent.
> c. If he is unable to alter the distress of the home parent while aspiring to do so; if he sees himself as more of a burden than a joy.
> d. If he is identified with the absent parent by the home parent or by the human relationship network, while that absent parent is devalued.
> e. If he is used as a mediating weapon between the parents.
> f. If he has no additional parent figure available when he is ready for it . . .
> g. If he has inadequate opportunities for reality testing about the absent parent. Such reality testing must include both the positive and the negative features of the real parent as the child experienced them and the child's own positive and negative feelings about this experience . . . (pp.554–555).

Although the literature suggests that the distress subsides after a year for most children, experience with children of divorce indicates that the divorce leads to subsequent problems with which the child must cope. The tasks of a child in a single-parent household are different from those of a child who has two parents at home. Parental dating and remarriage create stress for children. The latter frequently reawakens the immediate postdivorce adjustment behavior pattern because it signifies an end to the reconciliation fantasy which may have previously sustained the child. Parental remarriage underlines the finality of the divorce process. The adjustment to step-parents and further extended families presents another hurdle for these children who must negotiate major changes in the family system.

Growth Opportunities

The research generally has not addressed the issue of the possible positive effects of divorce, although Hetherington et al. (1977) concluded that a conflict-ridden intact family is more deleterious to family members than a stable home situation in which parents are divorced.

Weiss (1979) describes some positive effects on children of the changed household roles. The children are likely to be encouraged to be "more responsible, more independent, and more alert to adult values and concerns than are other children of the same age" (p.14). He also claims they are thrust to an earlier maturity and they learn to share the parent's worries, especially about money.

For young children, the precocious maturity and self-reliance may mask the genuine need for parental nurturance and support. Thus, on one hand, there is the pathogenic potential of precocious ego development. But, on the other hand there is the possibility of growth and the development of good coping mechanisms and an ability to deal with stress that will be carried forward in life.

For adolescents, the experience in a single-parent household allows greater independence than ordinarily available. Many adolescents are capable of assuming the responsibility and can seize the opportunity to develop their capacities and feel great self-satisfaction, particularly if the early years have provided an adequate nurturant foundation.

Conclusion

Wallerstein and Kelly (1980), in observing children of five years postdivorce note that "families that had a good outcome at five years were able to restabilize and restore the parenting after the initial, or sometimes extended, disorganization of the transition period" (p.215).

They concluded that the major detriment to children's well-being which divorce poses is the diminution or disruption of parenting.

Hess and Camara (1979) reached a similar conclusion when they compared children in divorced and intact families. Among the conclusions of their research are: "the family relationships that emerge after the divorce affect the children as much or more than the divorce itself" and "children's relationships to their parents are more significant to their adjustment than the level of discord between parents" (p.94).

An assumption of the authors of this book is that by focusing parents back on their parenting role, mental health professionals mitigate against the development of psychopathology in children by reducing the distress of the immediate post-divorce-related crisis periods and by increasing the likelihood of good parenting in the ensuing years.

Chapter 2

The Therapist and the Divorced Parent: When the Parent is the Client

Children need their parents for direction, support, discipline, limit setting, and love. But when a marriage falters and eventually breaks up, the partners in it are caught in their own emotional storm, focusing their energy inward on their own needs. Their children are frequently expected to fend for themselves. There are several reasons that this happens:

1. the children may be presumed to be unaware of what is happening or unaffected by it;
2. the parents may have no energy left for the children;
3. the parents may be uncomfortable communicating with the children about what is happening.

The children are placed under tremendous stress by the expectation that they can cope with the separation/divorce on their own. As they adjust to the changes in their lives, they need more support than usual. Some children appear to be coping successfully with their parents' divorce, but when they are given an opportunity to express themselves, in a group or individual counseling setting, their comments shed light on the difficulty they are having and their need for support.

> A 9-year-old boy, distraught that his father had left the home, reported to his group that he had told his 6-year-old brother: "Don't talk about Daddy in front of Mommy, because that will only make her cry more, and we'll have to cheer her up."

In his comment we can hear two statements: (1) his wish that his mother were under control and available to him, and (2) his feeling that he is taking on the role of the man of the family, with reluctance. Here is another example:

A 14-year-old girl commented to her therapist: "My father only calls to complain about how much money my mother is spending. Then they fight."

Behind her overt complaint about her parents' relationship is an indirect expression of her concern that her father is disinterested in her. What she has not verbalized is: My father never calls me.

Conveying the Message that You Are Still a Parent

We know that divorcing adults fare better when they have access to support networks. Studies have shown, for example, that the vulnerability of single parents to depression is compounded by the degree of social isolation (Longfellow, 1979). In response to this, groups such as "Parents Without Partners" have proliferated. Adults most often have friends who operate as a support system. Even attorneys, when called upon to handle divorce, become part of the adult's support system by providing guidance and encouragement.

But what about the children? There are no "Children with One-Parent" organizations. Their friends do not rush in to give them support. Indeed, many of them, especially during the latency period, never even tell their friends about the divorce because of their own feelings of shame associated with their parents' divorce or because their parents have told them to keep the divorce a secret. They rarely have lawyers to represent them in divorce proceedings. And, as previously observed, their parents are frequently not emotionally available to them to meet their increased needs and to reduce the stress.

The quality of parenting by both custodial and non-custodial parents is a crucial factor in the postdivorce life of a child and very much influences the child's adjustment. Recent research has indicated that longer term postdivorce adjustment is related to cumulative stress (Hodges et al., 1979) or the sustained conditions subsequent to the divorce event itself (Hess & Camara, 1979; Hetherington, 1979). Some of the factors involved in cumulative stress are: overt changes in lifestyle, such as moving; change of school and friends; and, change in economic circumstances. Changes in parenting are more covert, but nonetheless, observable. Among divorced mothers, poor parenting seems most marked one year after divorce (Hetherington et al., 1977). They have more difficulty coping with their children than do nondivorced parents. The difficulties are apparent in communication, discipline, and consistency. Sustained poor parenting places the child under stress. Therefore, it is of particular importance that divorcing parents be helped to refocus on their parenting role and to be good parents.

Optimally, the help would be forthcoming prior to or immediately upon the separation, in order to serve a preventive function. A preventive approach to mental health is preferable to an approach which seeks to rectify already existing problems. However, we recognize that in reality most parents do not present themselves or their children for help until a crisis is perceived. In order to bridge the gap between the ideal and the real, we recommend that mental health professionals take an activist position, lecturing before parent and professional groups, organizing and instituting programs in the community, and encouraging parents to seek help before a crisis emerges. In addition, therapists working individually with a divorced parent can refer the patient to a parenting group. School counselors who observe a counselee experiencing school difficulties can contact the parent and suggest the inclusion of the parent in a parenting group. Some years ago, Hawkins (1974) proposed universal parenthood training as part of the high school curriculum. The preventive notion embodied in the proposal has great merit.

Bellak (Bower, 1961) has commented that the governing of men and the raising of children are among the few vital occupations for which one does not have to certify minimum ability or previous training. In the same vein, Gordon (1971) noted that parents are blamed for the trouble that young people are having, but not trained for the demanding job of raising children. If parenting is a difficult task for the married parent who is ill-prepared for the task, it is even more so for the divorced parent because of the special problems of parenting created by divorce. Parents who are generally secure in their dealings with their children are more likely to be able to manage the additional parenting problems associated with divorce. In comparing children from single-parent families, regardless of whether mother or father had custody, those children whose parents were authoritative were found to be more socially competent than those whose parents were authoritarian or laissez-faire (Santrock & Warshak, 1979). The divorced parent who is secure in his or her role as parent and has the energy to attend to parenting will be most effective with the children.

The first task of the mental health professional who comes in contact with divorcing parents is to remind them that they are still parents. The next task is to provide them with the resources to be good parents. Whether in an individual or group therapy setting, the parents need to be helped to be firm, consistent, attentive, loving, encouraging, and reinforcing to their children and to separate problems with their spouses from their attitudes and behaviors towards their children.

Help-Seeking Behavior of Divorced Parents

Divorce is a stressful event in life. Individuals undergoing the stress vary in the ways in which they cope, choosing to handle it themselves or turning to others for support and guidance. Chiriboga, Coho, and Roberts (1979) reported on a study of the help-seeking behavior of 310 persons in the process of divorce. Not surprisingly, they reported that counselors, including social workers, psychiatrists and psychologists, were turned to with less frequency than friends or the spouse. They found a dramatic difference in the frequency with which men and women seek social support, with women being significantly more likely to do so. In addition, the study found age to be a significant variable, with younger people more likely to seek support than older people. They were surprised at the infrequency with which subjects chose self-help groups, preferring individual counseling. Kressel, Lopez-Morellas, Weinglass, and Deutch (1979) estimated that psychotherapy is sought in 20 to 30 percent of all middle-class divorces, with an upward trend possible. The implication of this research is that therapists are most likely to see younger women present themselves for help at the time of divorce. Mothers of young children can therefore be expected to be well represented, giving therapists an opportunity to intervene on behalf of the children.

The choice of the method for intervention will depend on several factors: (1) the training and orientation of the professional; (2) the needs and resources of the setting or institution in which the intervention takes place; and, (3) the parents' agreement to a modality which seems appropriate to their needs. We have found that when parent-child issues represent the presenting problem, parents are likely to either seek a parenting program or identify the child as the patient for individual counseling. They are least likely to present themselves for individual counseling to help them improve their parenting skills.

Wallerstein and Kelly (1977) placed the optimum intervention time for the children at between one and six months following parental separation. At that point, the chances for effecting change in a fluid system are enhanced. In addition, since many decisions regarding the children are made at that time, intervention provides an opportunity for consideration of consequences and alternatives. Wallerstein and Kelly developed a model of a 6-session child-centered, preventive counseling program for divorcing parents. They did not hold rigidly to the time limit and extended the intervention time when it appeared appropriate. The first task in the 6-session program was the clarification of goals that made clear that this was a prevention rather than a treatment program, not addressed to chronically disturbed children, but to those who were coping with a stressful event in their lives. Then, a careful, although telescoped, marital history was taken, which included a picture of the current situation and the place of the children. From the start, the parent was addressed in the parenting role so that parents would see the connections between the children's behavior and divorce induced stress.

By the third session, the therapist would have a tentative diagnostic formulation regarding the child's functioning, the parent's functioning, the parent-child relationship and other relationships in the child's environment, and could establish priorities for the counseling process. The therapists explicitly took a position advocating the children, and the counseling tended to be more advice giving and directive than the usual clinical pace. The approach was based on the assumption that the parents were capable of mature functioning in their role as parents.

The Choice of a Group Approach to Divorcing Parents

Group therapy makes use of psychotherapeutic techniques in a group setting, including the utilization of group interaction (Rowe, 1975). Although group therapies were first described in the 1940s, in the past decade, a number of variations emerged which focus on increasing self-understanding and providing support in times of stress.

A group approach may be particularly useful for divorced and separated parents because of the loneliness and lack of support a number of them experience. A group experience with other adults who have shared similar life stresses and experiences may be of particular benefit. Here, the parent has the opportunity to express feelings and discuss situations in a therapeutic and/or supportive environment. The therapist guides the group interaction in order to keep the setting *safe*, lending to a trusting atmosphere where disclosure will not bring on ridicule, sarcasm, or blame as might often be the case if the same information were presented to a friend or relative outside of the group.

Generally, the interaction for a group of divorced parents would be similar to the Situation/Transition (S/T) Model offered by Schwartz (1975). Such groups are primarily oriented towards helping members cope more effectively with a shared external event: they meet regularly over a period of weeks or months; they are led by a trained leader; they offer social support, factual information about the shared life stress, and an opportunity for emotional interaction with others around the group focus; and, they do not require members to espouse a particular moral or behavioral values system. In a group session, it is often comforting for adults to learn that others have experienced what they have experienced, felt what they have felt, and reacted as they have reacted. The group members often feel a sense of relief within the first few sessions knowing that they are *normal*. The group members may get advice from other group members based on the mutually shared experiences of loss of their marital relationship, single parenting, and attempts to begin new relationships. They can discuss the problems involved in raising children when there is conflict and disagreement with a former spouse, particularly around divorce-related issues such as custody, visitation, and payment of alimony and child support. For this reason, the divorced parent may find a homogeneous group more effective than a heterogeneous parent group in which married parents are also participants.

The groups which are probably most successful for the divorcing parent are based on a problem-solving model where coping skills and new methods for approaching stressful situations are learned. The group may then serve a valuable function of preventing serious problems from occurring in the adults themselves, in their children, or in the relationship between them.

Rationale for a Group Approach

The Opportunity for Mutual Support

Longfellow (1979) noted that social networks function to reduce some of the single mother's stress, but that divorced parents frequently experience a loss of their social networks as a consequence of the divorce. They complain that they feel uncomfortable among their married friends. They perceive their problems as divorced parents as being different from those of married parents. In addition, moving, seeking different or new employment, and losing the former spouse's kin system create additional losses of supportive people.

A group approach to divorced parents provides the members with an opportunity to establish a new support system from among the other participants, whom they see as like themselves. Hearing that other parents have the same or similar problems is reassuring. One mother in a group likened it to reading Dr. Spock when her children were babies: "If there was a paragraph about it in the book, then my child wasn't abnormal and I wasn't a bad mother." Arnold (1978) described this function of parent groups as providing parents with the opportunity to "count their blessings" by contrast or comparison with other parents.

The Economic Advantage of Group Therapy

To the individual. A common complaint of divorced persons is that they have less money available than they had when married. It costs more money for the former spouses to support two separate households than to support one. Even with insurance coverage, the cost to a client of a group experience is considerably less than the cost of individual therapy, whether it is sought from a private practitioner or from a community agency. Divorced parents are therefore more likely to perceive a group experience as something which they can afford. They are likely to view it as more cost effective than individual therapy.

To an agency. For an agency with limited professional resources available, a group for divorced parents is an economical way to serve the client population. A greater number of clients can be reached using fewer hours of professional time than individual or family approaches.

Parent Groups are Less Threatening

For many parents, a parent group offers an opportunity to accept advice about their children without a threat to their self-esteem. They can perceive themselves as interested, concerned parents, adding to their feelings of worth. Parents report that they like parenting programs and generally indicate that they are helped by them (Fine, 1980).

Success of Related Programs

Experience with groups for divorced individuals and with general parenting programs led to the development of the concept of groups for divorced parents, combining the benefits of both types of groups.

Types of group approaches to divorced individuals. There have been a number of reports in the literature of group approaches to divorced individuals, some of which include a focus on parenting. Although none of them identifies the program as an S/T group, they clearly follow the Schwartz model described earlier. The groups can have different formats to be determined by the orientation of the leader and by the goals of the group for the individuals included. For example, the groups may be structured or unstructured. In a structured group, the leader has an agenda. The sessions are planned with questions to be posed or topics to be discussed. An unstructured group is looser in organization with the group members deciding upon topics or group tasks as they proceed. There may be varying degrees of structure in a group.

Groups may be open or closed. An open group allows that as group members leave, they are replaced by new members to keep the group size constant. A closed group begins with a particular composition of group members and ends with those same members. Groups may be open-ended or time-limited. Open-ended groups can continue indefinitely with no date for the group termination. The time-limited group usually meets for eight to twenty sessions with the possibility of recontracting for an additional specified number of sessions. When the goals of the group are more educational than therapeutic, then a closed, time-limited group is preferable; whereas a group with more therapeutic goals lends itself to open membership and open-ended time frame.

Coche and Goldman (1979) described a 12-session group experience for divorced women. They chose a brief, closed group model in order to give members an opportunity to compare their experiences, gain confidence that the task is achievable, and acquire support in decision making. Nuclear conflict material was not dealt with in the groups. Issues confronted in the group included poor marriages, separation, and single parenting.

Nichols (1977) described a 4-part informational/educational series for divorced individuals. One of the sessions dealt with the problems of the children. Psychological factors such as children's guilt reactions, fears, and concerns over "being in the middle" were carefully explained. These groups were more like classes, in that they did not include group discussion, although participants did volunteer descriptions of how they dealt with practical problems.

Granvold and Welch (1977) described a Treatment Seminar, a 7-week series, with each successive session devoted to a different topic. One session was devoted to the impact of separation on the relationship with children. The Seminar applied cognitive-behavioral techniques to postdivorce adjustment problems.

Kressel and his colleagues (1979) noted that religious communities frequently offer group support to divorced parents, offering a reference group of similar-others and frequent social contacts.

Group approaches for improving parenting skills. Over the years, a number of parent education or parent counseling programs have been developed to teach parents more effective ways to deal with child rearing and child management problems. The St. Louis School Mental Health Project (Gildea, Glidewell, & Kantor, 1967) is an early example of a parent counseling program employing a discussion group. It originally sought to help parents deal with general problems in raising and educating children. Later, children with behavior problems were selected and their parents were invited to join a social worker in group therapy.

Hereford (1963) reported on a controlled study of the effectiveness of group discussion in changing parental attitudes and subsequently changing children's behavior. Discussion group parents showed significantly greater changes in attitudes and behavior than did a control group, and children whose parents attended improved significantly more in the degree of acceptance by classmates than did the control group.

Another group education technique that has received more popular acclaim than most parenting programs is Gordon's (1971) *Parent Effectiveness Training* (PET). The results of two doctoral studies of the effectiveness of PET lend support to Gordon's contention that PET changes parental attitudes, although subsequent changes in parental behavior or children's perception of their parent's acceptance is less certain (Cantor, 1976).

S. B. Gordon (1975) has reported on a Responsive Parenting class, a 10-week program for parents that includes a home project. Data from the home project indicated that actual changes in children's behavior had occurred as a result of their parents' participation in the program. All of these studies report on behaviorally oriented programs. In all likelihood, this is because, as Fine (1980) has suggested, outcomes of behaviorally oriented programs are easier to evaluate than are those of humanistically oriented programs, that look at changes in parent attitudes, beliefs, and values.

The *Parenting Skills: Trainer's Manual* (Abidin, 1975) presents a program designed to increase the chances that parents will be knowledgeable about the needs and development of children, and to give parents a range of specific skills in child rearing. In a study of its effectiveness as an intervention technique with parents of first grade children at risk, Cantor (1976) concluded that the program, reinforcing already interested parents in the direction of their concern, presented them with the opportunity to learn a new repertoire of skills and examine their own behavior as parents with the help of peers and a mental health professional.

The programs described above are designed to improve parenting skills, but do not take into account the additional stresses of the single parent or reconstituted family. A parenting program specifically designed to address the problems of divorced families can combine the two areas of general parenting skills and the additional stresses of divorce.

Models of Group Approaches to Divorced Parents

The goals of a group for divorced parents are to focus parents on their parenting role and to improve their skills as parents. The emphasis of the group may be primarily educational or primarily supportive. In an educational group, the meetings are structured by the leader, who has prepared material to present at each session. In a supportive group, the meetings are unstructured, with the subjects to be discussed emerging from material presented by the participants.

It is important, in either style of group, that parents understand from the outset that the leader will be co-advocating the children's position. The leader may, at times, encourage parents to put their needs aside or to reevaluate their needs in the light of the needs of the children. It is an assumption of the leader that parents have that obligation to their children.

Kessler (1978) studied the relative effectiveness of structured and unstructured divorce-adjustment groups. On a variety of measures, the structured groups were found to be more successful. Kessler hypothesized that the skill-building component of the structured group added to its effectiveness. In addition, the structured group may have encouraged a more active stance on the part of participants, as a result of exercises included in the program.

The Post-Divorce Parenting Program: A Structured Group Experience

The authors have developed a structured group program for divorced parents. It combines an educational approach with opportunities for participants to share their own experiences and to apply what they learn with their own children.

Intent of the program. The Post-Divorce Parenting Program (PDPP) is intended to help prevent, lessen, or remediate the difficulties children experience as a result of their parents' separation or divorce. The PDPP focuses parents' attention on the needs of the children. It educates parents about the best ways to handle divorce-related issues such as custody and visitation. It teaches parents skills and techniques of effective parenting and helps them apply the skills to specific problems associated with divorce. The PDPP, while sympathetic to the parents' personal needs, helps them refocus on their children. It is intended as a way of ameliorating stressful periods for the child during and following the separation/divorce.

The PDPP is different from other parenting programs in its specific focus on the problems associated with divorce. Because divorce places unique stresses on children and their parents, currently available parenting programs, such as PET (Gordon, 1971) or Parenting Skills (Abidin, 1975) which include general information in areas of parent-child communication or discipline, are insufficient to meet the needs of divorced parents and their children.

Design of the PDPP. The PDPP was devised to be presented in eight sessions of one-and-a-half hours each. Custodial and noncustodial parents were included in the group, because the program takes both perspectives into account. The group meets in a room large enough to comfortably accomodate the 8 to 12 participants. Age of children is not a crucial issue because the program is designed to consider problems involving children of all ages. The program includes an evaluative component, to be completed by the leader.

Format of the lessons: Each lesson provides educational material presented by the group leader, the opportunity for parents to respond with examples from their own experience, and small group exercises. The latter consists case examples, with incomplete endings. Parents are asked to respond to such questions as, "What do you think the child is communicating by that behavior?" or "What should the parent do now?" The group is divided into three or four subgroups to discuss the case material, decide upon answers, and report back to the large group. Case examples involve children at various age levels and the subgroups can be composed of parents whose children's ages correspond to the case material.

Each lesson includes a homework assignment that encourages the parent to apply the material that has just been presented. Homework is brought to the next group meeting, and some time at the beginning of each session is devoted to discussion of the previous assignment.

The 8 lessons of the program are:

1. *You are still a parent:* Introduces the parents to the leader, the program and each other, and establishes the goal of the program.
2. *How to be a good parent:* Presents general rules of good parenting, to serve as a framework for dealing with the specific problems associated with divorce.
3. *Four ways to minimize children's reactions to divorce:* Deals with some of the most common issues confronting divorced parents. This lesson is presented in full in Appendix A (see pp. 159–166) to provide the interested professional with a model of the PDPP.
4. *Handling children's emotional reactions to divorce, Part 1:* Describes the expected responses of preschool and early latency children and teaches parents how to respond to them.

5. *Handling children's emotional reactions to divorce, Part 2:* Describes the expected responses of later latency children and of adolescents and teaches parents how to respond to them.
6. *Handling custody and visitation problems:* Focuses on children's needs and teaches parents to separate their negative feelings toward the ex-spouse from custody and visitation decisions.
7. *Handling problems associated with parental dating and remarriages:* Helps parents to anticipate and understand the children's reactions.
8. *Dealing with one's own feelings about marriage, divorce and parenthood:* Helps parents to recognize their feelings and to express them in a way that will not be detrimental to the children.

Advantages of the PDPP. The structured, educational format of the PDPP ensures that a great deal of important material is presented to parents in a manner that makes economical use of resources. It is therefore especially appropriate for presentation in schools and community mental health centers.

Parents participating in the program have reported that they found the format unthreatening because they could assimilate the material without having to be any more personally revealing than they chose to be. For the professional leading the group, this means that the likelihood that a participant will be unable to cope with the stress of the group is minimal. Most participants in the PDPP have used the opportunity to share their personal experiences and concerns. The format of the program makes it relatively easy for the leader to keep the focus on the divorce-related issues and to keep other nuclear conflicts out.

A Supportive Group Approach

A less structured approach to divorced parents has also been found to be effective if the group leader keeps in mind that there still needs to be an educational component of the experience. There are principles of good parenting to be conveyed, as well as information about the effects of divorce on children and better ways of dealing with divorce-related issues. In this kind of group, the educational component is presented less formally than in the PDPP.

In a supportive group, the parents bring the material to the group, in the form of problems that they are having in dealing with their children. The other parents respond from their own experience. The group leader reinforces appropriate responses from participants, introduces other responses, explains why children may be behaving as they are, and explains why one response to the behavior is likely to be more effective than another.

The following excerpt from a supportive group illustrates this:

Parent A:	My ex-husband hasn't sent the child support payment this month, and he still expects to come and see the kids on Sunday. I'm going to call him and tell him he can't and if he won't listen, I'll just take the kids to my Mother's house on Sunday.
Parent B:	I don't blame you. I did the same thing. The only problem was, then my kids got mad at me for not letting them see their father. You'd think it was *my* fault!
Parent A:	I hadn't thought about that happening.
Parent C:	So what if they *are* mad? At least you'd get the money. Anyway, he doesn't deserve to see them.
Leader:	You all agree that it makes you angry when you don't receive your support payments. That's understandable. The problem is, that the anger is between you and your ex. The kids have nothing to do with it. We've talked about how it helps children to see the parent they don't live with as often as possible. Not letting them see that parent in a situation like this is punishing them and can be harmful to them.
	I wonder if anyone can suggest a way to Mrs. A. that she could resolve the child-support problem without involving the children?

The leader in a supportive group for divorced parents must be directive at times because there is a dual client: the parent who is present and the child who is not. If the leader is consistently nondirective, the children's needs are liable to be forgotten and the purpose of the group will have been undermined.

The Locale for a Group for Divorced Parents

There are a number of settings in which groups for divorced parents can be offered.

Schools

Schools provide an excellent opportunity for offering postdivorce parenting programs, for a number of reasons. Schools are present in every community and every child of divorce between ages 5 and at least 16 is in school. Parents are accustomed to relating to school personnel about their children. They perceive school personnel as knowledgeable and expert in matters concerning children. Schools employ the services of mental health professionals, including school psychologists, social workers, and counselors, who are potential group leaders. Schools are constantly communicating with parents via flyers, notices, and PTA newsletters. Therefore, they have available a mechanism for disseminating information about the availability of groups.

Finally, since schools cannot effectively educate children who are suffering the ill effects of divorce and/or poor parenting, it is appropriate to use school personnel to run groups for divorced parents as a means of reaching the children and improving their receptivity to learning. Mental health professionals in schools will have to approach the administrators and convince them of the importance of using their services in this way. The authors have made presentations to state associations of school administrators in an effort to convince them to institute special services for children of divorce, including groups for divorced parents, groups for the children, and training programs for school personnel.

Community Mental Health Centers (CMHC)

The Community Mental Health Services Act of 1975 (Public Law 94–63) specified children as a mandated target population to be served by community mental health centers, both directly and indirectly. Groups for divorced parents provide indirect service to children. By educating and consulting with parents, the needs of the children are served.

School administrators may be reluctant to use their personnel to serve parents, in spite of the rationale offered above. However, community mental health center administrators can be expected to cooperate in the development of group programs for divorced parents as an appropriate service to be offered. Parents are likely to look to these agencies for help and are frequently referred to them by school personnel.

Cantor (1978) recommended that schools and CMHCs cooperate in serving the needs of children of divorce. She suggested that the schools serve as a site for groups for the children, and that the leader work in conjunction with the leader of the parent group meeting in a CMHC to coordinate the content of the parent group with needs expressed by the children. Drake (1978) described the role of an educator-clinician hired by a CMHC, whose role is to serve as a link between the CMHC and schools in the community. Educator-clinicians can coordinate the efforts of the two settings. They may choose to coordinate the parent and the children's groups by running both themselves or by training personnel in either setting to run the groups and then serve as liaison between the group leaders.

Private Practitioners

There are many therapists who are known in their communities and among their professional colleagues for their work with groups. For such individuals to run groups specifically for divorced parents is logical and practical. Once they let it be known that the groups are available, client self-referral and referral from colleagues is likely.

Group therapists who are unaccustomed to running time-limited groups or Situation/Transition groups with a topic focus might have to modify some of their usual procedures. However, they also have the opportunity to use their skills to broaden the scope of the group experience to encompass other conflicts. Private practitioners have the greatest opportunity for flexibility in offering groups to divorced parents. The constraints of time, space, and personnel that are present in public settings are less of a problem in private practice. There is a group of potential clients who prefer to seek help in the private sector and their needs can be met well by privately practicing professionals.

Other Settings

Religious institutions can offer parenting programs for divorced parents. Kressel and his colleagues (1979) reported that when people seek help with a marital problem, they are more likely to turn to a member of the clergy than a psychotherapist. For many people, seeking help from a psychotherapist still has negative connotations. By offering the group experience through a religious organization, the "halo effect" of the setting is capitalized upon. Clergy with training as pastoral counselors are potential group leaders, as are mental health professionals who come into the religious institution.

A model of a church-affiliated group program is the seminar series, "Preserving Parent-Child Relationships in Changing Families." This series of four classes was led by a psychologist from the local child guidance clinic and sponsored by the Stamford, Connecticut Deanery. After the four classes, parents continued to attend a series of seven weekly discussions (Rozhon, 1980).

Adult schools and college extension programs are another prime location for postdivorce parenting programs. The adult schools already have a locale for the group and an administrative procedure for advertising and registering. There is no social stigma attached to taking a course at an adult school. On the contrary, it is looked upon favorably. Mental health professionals need to propose these programs to the adult schools or colleges, describing the need, usefulness, and potential response of the target audience. Because adult schools and extension programs generally have to be financially self-sustaining, the community needs and anticipated response are crucial factors to be considered in proposing programs to these institutions.

Parents Without Partners (PWP)

Since PWP already exists to serve the needs of divorced and other single parents, it appears to be an excellent setting to sponsor postdivorce parenting programs. Mental health professionals, recognizing the need for these programs, need to approach local PWP groups and devise mutually satisfying means by which the programs can be offered.

In Cooperation with the Courts

A model exists in Los Angeles for a court-sponsored postdivorce counseling service (Elkin, 1977). It is available to families returning to court for postdivorce litigation regarding custody and/or visitation problems. In Maricopa County, Arizona (Maricopa County Bar Association, 1980), a Conciliation Court has been established, providing free-of-charge professional counseling. The purpose of the counseling is to encourage communication between the couple prior to the divorce. It also provides postdissolution counseling regarding custody and visitation problems.

In the future, it would be extremely beneficial if courts could sponsor parenting programs for families coming before them in the divorce process. In New Jersey, where a bill is being considered to make joint custody the presumed arrangement, the New Jersey Association for the Advancement of Psychology has recommended that a counseling process be written into the law, as a means of increasing the likelihood that the joint custody arrangement will be successful. The expense to the court of such programs may well preclude their inception, unless we can demonstrate the huge benefit to society in terms of the effectiveness of a primary prevention model.

Group Leaders

The Code of Ethics of the American Psychological Association states: "The Psychologist recognizes the boundaries of his or her competence and the limitations of his/her techniques and does not offer services or use techniques that fail to meet professional standards established in a particular field." This provides a model for the ethics of leadership for a group for divorced parents.

In keeping with the Code of Ethics, the leader of a group for divorced parents needs to be well prepared in three areas: (1) group leadership and the dynamics of groups; (2) parenting training; and (3) the specific problems associated with divorce and parenting. Appendix B includes a bibliography for professionals who wish to further increase their knowledge in the latter two areas prior to embarking on the leadership of a group for divorced parents.

Most groups for divorced parents are not psychotherapy groups, although their outcome can be therapeutic. The distinction rests on the focused nature of the subject of the group, the exclusion of nonrelated subjects from the group, and the fact that participants' resistances and defenses are not generally interpreted. Nevertheless, group members frequently are getting more from the experience than appears on the surface and may even be using the common experience as a metaphor for deeper issues (Schwartz, 1975). We see mental health professionals as the appropriate leaders of these groups because of their skills and expertise, including their training to run groups.

In groups for divorced parents, the leader is usually perceived as an expert, a kind of superparent to whom the members can turn for answers. The leader can use the perception to model good parenting behavior; reinforcing parents, encouraging them to trust their own judgment when appropriate, and acknowledging that he or she doesn't have an answer all the time and may have been wrong.

Limitations and Cautions

Parental Pathology

Although the group for divorced parents is supportive and educational in nature, it may still produce its casualities. Any group experience has the potential for adversely affecting its members. It is important that the group leader, from the outset, be alert to the possibility that some groups members have psychopathology that makes them inappropriate as participants. The group leader must let the individual know why the parent group might be uncomfortable or even harmful and should refer the individual for psychotherapy. Severely depressed individuals or those with indications of psychotic thinking are inappropriate to the group programs that have been discussed. Occasionally, an individual's pathology is less blatant, but the vulnerability is evident when the material being discussed or the nature of the interaction among group members triggers an inappropriate reaction. Here, the group leader has the task of first reducing the person's distress and then recommending another source for help with the problem.

> Mrs. A. had been a quiet observer in a supportive group for divorced parents. She never presented her own problems for consideration by the group and rarely offered suggestions to the other participants. Her affective responses were minimal. Yet,

she returned week after week, apparently getting something from her participation in the group. At the sixth meeting, a sharp, loud exchange took place between two group members who disagreed about the way to deal with a child's behavior. Mrs. A. covered her ears and began to cry, "Stop! Stop!"

The group members were startled. The Leader drew Mrs. A. aside, calmed her down, and asked her to stay at the end of the session. At that point, the Leader and Mrs. A. explored her associations to what had been happening between the other two group members. Mrs. A. related it to her own parents' fights. The Leader suggested that if Mrs. A. still responded so strongly to something from her own childhood, she might do well to see a therapist herself to deal with her own problems. The Leader pointed out that the Parenting Group only dealt with the children's difficulties. Mrs. A. welcomed the suggestion and did seek individual counseling.

Special Issues in Childrearing

The group is an arena for discussing problems and situations that are common to divorced parents. Sometimes a parent has another agenda that is not of interest to the other group members. Among those that have emerged in groups for divorced parents are the special problems of adopted children and handicapped children. The group leader has to judge whether these issues are distracting from the task of the group as a whole. If they are, the leader has two obligations: one is to the group to bring the focus back to areas of general interest; and the second one is to the individual with the special problem to respond to the concern. The parent with a special problem may be referred to another source that responds to that particular problem or may be referred for some individualized counseling. For some groups, it may be feasible to add a session to deal with pre-existing circumstances that complicate the resolution of the divorce trauma.

Keeping the Focus on the Children

Divorced parents have numerous other problems associated with divorce, including financial concerns, loneliness, and their own sexuality. It is, therefore, a hazard of a divorced parents' group, particularly of the supportive less structured group, that the focus will slip away from parenting to other issues. The group leader needs to be alert to what is happening and to interpret the behavior in helpful terms, such as, "We know how difficult it is when you have concerns of your own to concentrate on the children, even here."

Summary

A group model for reaching divorced parents is economical, practical, and effective as a tool for educating parents in childrearing skills and teaching them to deal with the special problems of children of divorce. Groups can be housed in a variety of settings: schools, community mental health centers, adult schools, or the offices of private practitioners.

A mental health professional with training in running groups and knowledge about parenting and the impact of divorce is an optimal group leader, able to keep the focus on the task at hand and prepared to deal with any unexpected turn of events.

Parents who have had the benefit of a group experience come away from it with (in addition to knowledge acquired and specific suggestions) a support group of individuals who have shared a common life stress.

The Choice of Individual Treatment

The services of mental health professionals are frequently sought by people contemplating separation in order to help them through the decision-making process or subsequent to the separation to deal with the ensuing pain. If the client is also a parent, we believe that it is incumbent upon the therapist, regardless of theoretical orientation, to consider the impact on the children and to make child-centered interventions. The therapist and client should make a specific agreement at the outset that benefit to the children is a goal of therapy. The therapist who perceives this as anathema and contrary to doing good therapy has an obligation to refer the patient elsewhere for parent counseling.

The patient referred for individual treatment is frequently the child. When this is the case, and the child is preschool, latency age or preadolescent, we recommend that the parent be seen concurrently by the same therapist. This is true as well when a child from an intact family is referred for therapy. The underlying assumption is that the parents and the home environment have contributed to and reinforce the child's emotional problems and that without the parents' insight and willingness to change, the task of getting better may be insurmountable for the child. In addition, parents are a valuable source of information about the child. With young children, Gardner (1976) recommends working with the parent in the room as an observer and occasional contributor.

When the referred patient is an adolescent, we often recommend that a parent be seen in concurrent treatment by another therapist. In this way, the confidentiality of the relationship between the adolescent client and the therapist is maintained, while the parent is also receiving therapy and being educated to be a better parent. Consultation between the two therapists, with the clients' permission, is helpful.

Sometimes the stress of being a single parent will serve as the impetus to seeking individual therapy. When this is the case, the focus of the therapy sessions is the parent-child relationship.

When the client is a divorced parent, the therapist has to listen to the material with an ear toward how the children are being affected. The therapist needs to co-advocate the child's position. This is a relatively easy task if the child has been identified as the patient. Then the parent expects comments and interventions on the child's behalf. However, when the parent is the identified patient, the therapist who advocates the child's position has a more sensitive task. The therapist has to be able to take into account the parent's needs as well as the child's, and help the parent to recognize the point at which those needs conflict. The parent has to understand what is being recommended and must be willing to cooperate (Arnold, 1978). When the therapist advocates the child's position, he or she may become the object of parental hostility. However, the hostility itself can be effectively worked with. It can serve, for example, as a vehicle for recognizing the parent's competitiveness with the child in seeking attention.

Working Therapeutically with a Divorced Parent

The therapist working with a divorced parent, whether the parent has sought help for himself or for the child, needs to be cognizant of a number of factors in relation to the children.

Parenting Problems Do Not Exist in a Vacuum

The kinds of difficulties that parents have with their children reflect the parents' own conscious and unconscious needs. When the parents' needs are unconscious, they need to be understood and resolved in the course of therapy. Otherwise, although the parents may follow the therapist's advice by rote and be helpful to the children in that way, they are likely to find other ways to continue to meet their neurotic needs in the parent-child relationship.

> Mrs. B. brought her 8-year-old daughter in for treatment because the child was still bed-wetting. The therapist saw Mrs. B. and the child concurrently. Mrs. B. and the therapist explored the ways

Mrs. B. had used to discourage the child from bed-wetting. Mrs. B. realized that she had done nothing. Indeed, Mrs. B. discovered that she had an unconscious desire to keep her daughter infantilized for several reasons, including her desire to be young herself. She identified with the nurturance that the infant/child received, and had doubts concerning her ability to parent an adolescent by herself.

The therapist could have provided Mrs. B. with specific techniques to end the child's bed-wetting behavior. However, if Mrs. B. still had an unconscious need to infantilize the child, she would have continued to do so in other ways.

Many divorced parents behave in ways that are deleterious to their children in order to consciously retaliate against the ex-spouse. In such instances, the therapist needs to point out the harmful effects on the children and to help the parent work out the feelings toward the ex-spouse in ways that do not involve the children.

Impact of the Parents' Present Psychological Functioning on the Children

Studies have shown that divorced and separated mothers are more likely to have psychiatric symptoms than married mothers (Longfellow, 1979). A depressed or hostile parent is unlikely to be able to suspend those feelings in relationship to the children. Consequently, positive changes in the parent's psychological functioning will increase parenting capacity (Wallerstein & Kelly, 1977).

When a divorced parent is exhibiting psychiatric symptoms, they must be dealt with in therapy prior to considering the parent-child interaction because they constitute an obstacle to a healthy parent-child relationship. The parent will not be responsive to suggestions for improving the parent-child relationship until there is an improvement in his or her own emotional state, as in the case of Mrs. C.:

Mrs. C. presented herself for therapy subsequent to separation from her husband. She recognized that her behavior, especially an extramarital affair, had precipitated the separation that she had thought she wanted. Nevertheless, she was clinically depressed. She spent most of her time in bed or lying on the couch in front of the television. She described herself as being without energy, unable to get up. She cried a great deal of the time. Her sons, ages 9 and 6, were fending for themselves. They prepared TV dinners and were responsible for their baths, bedtime, and all after-school entertainment. Fortunately for the children, Mrs. C.'s mother became aware of the situation and began coming over after school to take care of them.

Mrs. C. entered a private mental hospital for a brief period. The florid symptoms of the depression were treated biochemically and she was able to function moderately well. Continued psychotherapy gradually reduced the depression and as it did, she became increasingly available to mother the children. Only then did parenting issues enter into the treatment.

Pathological involvement of parents with their children. Therapists need to be alert to unconscious substitution of the children for the ex-spouse in supporting neurotic or narcissistic needs of the parents. When it becomes apparent that parental needs are being met by the children, the client must explore the needs, understand them, and give them up or change the way in which they are being gratified. If this is not accomplished before the therapist recommends a change in parental behavior towards the child, the parent is unlikely to cooperate in making the change.

Mrs. D. had presented herself for individual treatment because of her feelings of depression subsequent to her husband's leaving. She reported to her therapist that she had invited her six-year-old son to share her bedroom with her. She acknowledged that she felt abandoned and lonely and the presence of the child relieved those feelings.

The therapist knew that the arrangement was unhealthy for the child. But before Mrs. D. could understand that the current sleeping arrangement was harmful to her son and move him back to his own room, she had to work on her own feelings of loneliness and her ways of dealing with it. When this had been accomplished, Mrs. D. readily accepted the therapist's recommendation regarding the sleeping arrangement.

If the parent is unwilling to explore his or her own neurotic needs, then the child is likely to be caught up in them until he or she is old enough to be responsible for the change.

Diane was a 16-year-old whose parents had divorced when she was 14. She was in individual treatment because she had been involved in some minor delinquent behavior.

Diane had requested that her father assume custody of her, because she perceived him as the more warm and giving of her parents. When Diane moved in, she was given a list of chores and responsibilities. It soon became evident to her that her father was going to meet few of her needs, but was going to use her to meet his. Diane reported to her therapist that she had told her mother what was happening. Her mother had confided that she had left her husband because that was just the way he had treated her.

Diane's therapist arranged a conference with the father and Diane, the goal of which was to refer him for therapy to explore his behavior. He refused because he was not uncomfortable with his behavior.

Diane and her therapist worked through her feelings of rejection and anger and Diane began to look elsewhere to have her own needs for affection and warmth satisfied.

Parental naiveté. Many parents who come for individual treatment are naive and uninformed regarding general rules of good parenting and how to handle the specific problems associated with divorce. The therapist cannot assume that parents know how to handle their children and therefore the therapist needs to take on an educational role.

Mrs. E. presented herself for therapy when her husband left her. She had two boys, ages 10 and 8. Mrs. E. was furious with her husband for leaving, and consciously chose to punish him by denying him access to the children. Before dealing with Mrs. E.'s anger, the therapist educated her regarding the children's need to see their father and suggested that the subsequent therapeutic task would be to find other ways of expressing anger and to explore the need to stay angry. Mrs. E. said she was willing to accept the directive because she would be able in her therapy to talk about the anger. The implication was that if she were not in therapy and was told to let the children see their father, she would not have consented.

Advantages of Individual Counseling for Divorced Parents

Individual counseling provides an opportunity for working with more than the specific divorce-related problems. It permits the client to examine other nuclear conflicts and to ameliorate a broader range of symptoms and psychopathology. In contrast to parent group programs, individual counseling focuses on the specific needs of the client.

For adults, as for children, one of the important variables in postdivorce adjustment is predivorce adjustment. Many parents who blame the divorce for their symptoms and psychopathology may well have been only moderately defended before the divorce. The stress of divorce weakens the defenses. When counseling only deals with the postdivorce problems, their root may be ignored and they would be likely to reappear during the next life stress.

Examples of Individual Counseling with Divorced Parents

In each of the individual counseling cases that follow, the parent dealt with many issues and conflicts in therapy. However, we have extracted materials in which matters directly pertaining to the children came up in the treatment. Frequently, it related to the parents' other problems, with the children serving as a focus of the neurotic behavior.

The authors recognize that the cases presented are neither exhaustive nor inclusive of techniques used in practice. However, the cases offer examples of the ways in which parenting issues are brought into the treatment situation, and the therapist's responsibility to educate parents and to consider the child's needs simultaneously with the parents.

A Mother Deciding on Separation

One of the crucial times at which individuals seek counseling is when the decision to separate is being considered. Gardner (1978) advises therapists not to offer advice, but rather to help the client clarify the situation, feelings, and needs as much as possible so that the most judicious decision can be reached. The children are frequently an issue in the decision-making process, as in the case of Mrs. F.

> Mrs. F. was a 45-year-old mother of three: a boy, age 13, and two girls, ages 15 and 8. She had been married for 20 years to a self-employed attorney. She had been employed as a decorator during most of her marriage and her earnings were comparable to those of her husband. In the year prior to seeking help, Mrs. F. had become involved with a married man who worked with her. She found him to be far more communicative, understanding, and sexually interesting than her husband. She described the marital relationship as revolving around mutual interest in the children.
>
> Mrs. F. had a number of concerns to deal with in making her

decision. One was her strong religious background that frowned upon divorce. Related to that was her anticipation of the anger and dismay which her mother would display to her, and her longstanding need to please her mother. She also expressed reluctance to hurt her husband, whom she described as "the guy in the white hat," a person whom everyone saw as terrific and doing everything right. Indeed, it was his acts of omission rather than commission that had led her to seek the attention and affection of another man.

Finally, Mrs. F. was sincerely interested in the impact a divorce would have upon her children. She actively worked with her feelings about them and sought information and advice from her therapist, especially as she resolved the previously mentioned problems and moved closer to making the decision to separate.

Early in her therapy, Mrs. F. expressed concern about her older daughter.

Mrs. F.:   If I break up this home, what happens? They've had love and discipline. It's heartbreaking. A young girl might become promiscous.
Therapist: What makes you think that?
Mrs. F.:   Because she'd need a lot of attention or get bored. She might get into trouble. She'd get pregnant. You hear about that. It might happen because she had a mother who didn't care as a punishment to the mother.
Therapist: There seem to be two issues: Your feelings of guilt and with that, your need to be punished, and whether you could still show your daughter you cared about her if you left her father.
Mrs. F.:   I think I could. I mean, I wouldn't go far away. I'd still be there for her; to go shopping or to see her teachers or to drive her around. I might even be around more because I wouldn't have to manufacture time to see my boyfriend. I guess the important thing is that I still be available to her and the other kids if I leave my husband.
Therapist: That is important.

The session continued with the focus on Mrs. F.'s guilt feelings and her projection onto her daughter of her feelings about herself.

Some months later, Mrs. F. had begun to broach the subject of separation with her husband.

Mrs. F.:	He said he is not going anywhere. I said, "Should I? What about the kids? Are you saying that if I go I can take the kids?" He didn't answer me. So it went. There was no satisfaction. I guess the kids are important to both of us. The family is what makes the relationship between us.
Therapist:	Neither of you wants to lose the children but you're afraid that one of you will have to.
Mrs. F.:	Sure. He won't leave the house. So if I go, I lose the kids because they'll stay in the house with him. I can't give them up.
Therapist:	I wonder if you and your husband have considered joint custody.
Mrs. F.:	No. I just assumed one of us would have them. How could we arrange joint custody?
Therapist:	From what you've said, it seems as if both of you care deeply about the children and want to continue to parent. You and your husband also seem to be able to talk about the children's welfare without arguing and you each agree that the other is a good parent. Perhaps you can discuss it together and work out a way that you both continue to share parenting even if you're separated.

Mrs. F. and her husband did work out a mutually satisfactory agreement. She rented a house a few blocks from her home. The children would spend two months in each house with free access to the other at all times. The move back and forth would necessitate no change in school or friends for the children.

When Mr. and Mrs. F. had clarified the arrangements themselves, they came in together for a session with Mrs. F.'s therapist to talk about telling the children their plans. The therapist recommended that they both tell the children. Mr. and Mrs. F. decided that the older two should be told at the same time and the youngest should hear it separately because she needed a different explanation more appropriate to her age. At the next session:

Mrs. F.:	We told the kids. My son and my little daughter are okay, but my big daughter is having difficulty. I'll have to keep talking with her. Fifteen is such a sensitive age! Anyway, we're all talking and we're using a lot of humor to get over the rough spots.
Therapist:	What do you think is going on with your daughter?

Mrs. F.:   I think she's just disillusioned—you know, if this could happen to my parents, whom can I trust? She's hard to reach. She keeps so much inside. The little one came right out with the questions when we told her, and she comes back every time she thinks of another one. My son had gotten his father's ear. But I think I'm going to have to pursue my older daughter. I know from my own experience that it doesn't help to hold it all in.

The plans to separate and share custody were successfully effected. Subsequently, Mr. and Mrs. F. each remarried, but the custody arrangements remained the same. At the point at which Mrs. F. terminated therapy, all three children were reportedly succeeding in school, in extracurricular areas, and with their respective peers.

A Custodial Father

A custodial father who has previously assumed a traditional role in the family has particular problems in adjusting to being the primary parent. In the case of Mr. G., the problem was exacerbated by the fact that he assumed custody after having been out of the home for seven years.

Mr. G. was a 42-year-old man who had been divorced for seven years. His wife, who had custody of their three children, ages 19, 17, and 15, lived in another part of the country. She had decided that she could not retain custody because she had been unemployed for a year. Mr. G. agreed to have the two younger children come to live with him for one year. The eldest child was away at college. After two months of the new arrangement, Mr. G. presented himself for therapy. His youngest son, Paul, was unhappy, sullen, and unresponsive in school. The guidance counselor had suggested counseling for Paul, who refused it, so Mr. G. decided to seek help.

Mr. G. saw a parent as a physical caretaker only. Consequently, he fixed breakfasts and dinners, did the laundry, and kept the apartment clean, but rarely spoke with the boys, except to gather information, such as what they wanted for dinner or where they were going after school. Early in treatment, it became apparent that his style with his ex-wife was similar and that he rarely expressed his wishes or thoughts, passively letting things happen. The therapeutic goal for Mr. G. was to open him to his feelings, particularly where they interfaced with his sons. Thus, the context for treatment was frequently the parent-child relationship.

At the second session, Mr. G. reported that Paul was concerned about going back to visit his mother during the summer, wondering about whether or not he would come back.

Therapist: What is your custody agreement?
Mr. G.:   We have joint legal custody; but she had physical custody. We made an exception to that because we felt it was in the children's best interest to be with me now in this community.
Therapist: You seem vague about the permanence of this arrangement.
Mr. G.:   We've always been sort of vague. If she had the income to have Paul with her, I probably wouldn't resist. I've let her call the shots. I've been the last resort. Mom is the more popular one. It wasn't their free choice to relocate.
Therapist: What would *you* like?
Mr. G.:   I'd like Paul to live with me. But that seems selfish— you know, wanting to have more for myself.
Therapist: I wonder if Paul knows that you feel that way about having him around.

Mr. G. reported at the next session that he had told Paul how he felt. Paul had been surprised. He thought his father hated having him there.

Several weeks later, Mr. G. heard from the school that Paul had been suspended for three days because he left the building at lunchtime with some friends.

Therapist: How did you react?
Mr. G.:   I reviewed the importance of being in school. I guess I lectured him.
Therapist: What would it be like to talk *with* him rather than lecture *at* him?
Mr. G.:   I've got a lot of fear. I think it goes back to my relationship with my Mom and Dad when I was a kid. I'm so fearful of things flaring up. It was so rare that things were good and happy. With my wife, it was the same thing. So if I confront things, I'll turn off a relationship. I even get their breakfast because

I'm afraid if I told them to do it, they might not and then I'd have to confront them.

Therapist: And?

Mr. G.: If I flare up then the other person will and I won't be able to cope. I'd withdraw. Or else I might shout and throw something. I'd like to shout and rant and rave——

Therapist: You're afraid to let your feelings become that intense.

Mr. G.: I think I'm afraid I'd go crazy.

Mr. G. began communicating with Paul. At first, he opened up about the past, about his relationship with his own parents and what had happened in his marriage. He realized that he was not confronting Paul or dealing with their relationship, but he saw himself laying the groundwork by sharing his thoughts and feelings about other subjects. He observed that Paul was spending less time alone in his room reading. Paul was seeking Mr. G.'s company. Gradually, without Mr. G. having to lecture him about the importance of being out with peers, Paul began to make weekend plans.

Later the focus of Mr. G.'s therapy shifted.

Mr. G.: I want to continue talking with you about a number of things I've disclosed. You know, in talking, there's a sense of relief. I realize I came here originally to talk about Paul and my relationship with him. That served as a catalyst. Now I realize I've got to get myself straightened out.

At the end of the school year, Paul returned to his mother. Before he left, he and Mr. G. were able to talk about their feelings.

Mr. G.: Paul is the sweetest guy in the world. He's worried about going back to his old high school and how he'll relate there to his peers. Will he be able to get back into the circle? I told him I think he will. He's grown and matured this year. I told him I wish he'd come back here—that he means too much for me to say, "Sorry, you've burned your bridges."

Therapist: You seem a little hurt by his leaving.

Mr. G.: I am. I finally got close to someone and he's leaving. But at least I had the closeness and I've told him how I feel.

Mr. G. continued in therapy for another year. He met a woman during that time and was able to develop an intimate relationship with her. He stayed in close contact with Paul, visited frequently, and reported that Paul was doing well socially and academically.

A Custodial Mother

Custodial mothers present themselves for individual therapy for several reasons. Sometimes the stress of single parenting becomes overwhelming. In other instances, one or more of the children begins to show signs of distress and the mother presents herself to help the children. The therapist should initially accept the parent's perception of the presenting problem, even if it seems obvious that the children are being used as a way for the parent to get help. As therapy proceeds, the shift to the parent's needs will be accomplished as the connections between the children's difficulties and the parent's are interpreted.

Mrs. H., a 35-year-old custodial mother of two, who has been divorced for two years, presented herself for counseling because she felt that her relationship with her 8-year-old son, Larry, was poor. Her 4-year-old daughter was severely retarded. Her ex-husband had just accused Larry of taking some money. She had tried discussing it with Larry, but was unsuccessful in getting Larry to talk with her. They had never talked about Larry's feelings about the divorce or about his father, whom Mrs. H. perceived as unreliable and frequently disappointing to the children. The therapist suggested that Mrs. H. begin by reading *The Boys and Girls Book about Divorce* (Gardner, 1970) with Larry, selecting chapters that seemed germane.

Mrs. H. reported at the next session that she had read two chapters of the book to Larry.

Mrs. H.: Larry listened and got sad. He wanted to talk but he didn't want to. All he said was, "I've given up." It was upsetting to me. I want him to talk more.

Therapist: You seem impatient for him to change.

Mrs. H.: Funny that you say that. My parents are here. They're driving me crazy. I realized that I do to Larry just what my father did to me. I always had to get something right away. I tried when I was little. I wanted his approval. Then, as a teenager, I gave up and became the rebel. I don't like the idea that I'm as controlling of Larry as my parents were of me.

Therapist: How do you see yourself as controlling with Larry?

Mrs. H.:	When he's angry with me, I feel I've lost control. I *do* need to control situations, or I get scared.
Therapist:	Scared?
Mrs. H.:	That he'll go ape and be an undisciplined person. A person needs to learn limitations.
Therapist:	You're scared that if you were to lose control, you'd go ape.
Mrs. H.:	I saw my sister go ape. She practically abandoned her children. It was so frightening to see her out of her head.
Therapist:	So everyone's anger has to be kept in check. Everyone has to be under control.

Several weeks later, after more work had been done with issues around anger and loss of control, the following took place in a session:

Mrs. H.:	Some things have happened with Larry that are kind of exciting. Over the weekend, he said, "If Martha (the 4-year-old sister) is dead when you come back, I'll have to die." I asked why and he told me it was because he'd have killed her. He's accepting his anger at having a retarded sister because I'm accepting it from him. Then he told me later about a fight he had with a friend of his. Imagine Larry having a fight! And he told me all kinds of gory things he wished he could do to the kid. And finally, he told me he was mad at his father for not showing up on Sunday.
Therapist:	You seem very pleased.
Mrs. H.:	I am. Look what was happening and no one lost control—not Larry, not me! It's terrific. I had a dream—something about inflicting harm on my ex. I must have really been angry!

As Mrs. H. worked through her own angry feelings, understanding the difference between wanting to do something and actually doing it, she was able to tolerate Larry's anger. She also felt less guilty about Larry's anger at his father which she had previously regarded as a projection of her own anger.

| Mrs. H.: | I find it easier to talk about what Larry says about Martha than what he says about his father. I don't pursue things with Larry about his father. Larry says I'm afraid of his father. (crying) It's hard to talk |

about him. If I really say what I feel—that his
father's a bastard and left because we had a retarded
child. I can't say, "I hate him. I can't stand his guts."
I kept these feelings in for too long. I can't deal with
the way he abandoned me emotionally. I hate him. I
considered getting a hit man to kill him. I don't see
how my feelings can change. (silence—long pause).

Therapist: How are you feeling now?

Mrs. H.: Relieved. I never said those things to anyone.

About three months later, Mrs. H. reported the following:

Mrs. H.: Larry did something interesting on Sunday. He
threw out a lot of old junk.

Therapist: What did you find interesting?

Mrs. H.: I think it was significant—that he could let go of his
old ways—that he's able to grow up. It's kind of
nice.

Mrs. H. continued in individual therapy, to complete her own
task of growing up. Larry continued to have occasional difficulties with his father, but he could turn to his mother for some
support when he couldn't handle the situation on his own.

A Noncustodial Mother

Mrs. I. sought therapy after she had made the decision to leave
her husband. She was experiencing strong feelings of guilt in
anticipation of leaving her three children, particularly the
youngest, 13-year-old Jenny. Her concern for Jenny stemmed
from the fact that she had been having some difficulties in school.
She had been reported several times recently for cutting class and
smoking, and was in danger of academic failure. Mrs. I. was
certain that Jenny was aware of her intention to move out of the
house and that her behavior was designed to keep her there.

Mrs. I.: I can't wait to get out of there. When three o'clock
comes, I can't keep my cool. Jenny comes home and
if she's angry about anything, she yells at me. I can't
be superperson. I may respond in kind. But you
know, since we told the kids that I'll be leaving as
soon as I find an apartment, I can tolerate more from
Jenny.

Therapist: What do you see as the reason?

Mrs. I.: I'm less anxious and uptight. I think I used to take

out on Jenny all my anger at Jack (her husband). I
don't feel so stuck now—so I'm not as angry.

I realize that Jenny is testing me. I told her I'm
not responsible for her school work. She made it
sound like I don't care. I tell her I do care, but I won't
fight.

Therapist: Fighting was your way of showing interest in Jenny.
She is not used to the change.

Mrs. I.: I guess that's why she keeps hassling me. I won't
fight and she hates it.

Therapist: What has replaced the fighting in your relationship
with her?

Mrs. I.: I don't know. I've really disengaged. I wonder if I'm
practicing being alone. Maybe I've gone too far.

Mrs. I. began to look at other ways of relating to Jenny. She
realized that she never demonstrated affection or praised her and
she began doing both. Jenny's attitude toward her showed a
marked improvement. Mrs. I. found an apartment close to the
family home and she moved into it by herself. The children were
each given a key and Mr. and Mrs. I. were able to agree to a
completely open visitation policy. A meeting with lawyers
aroused some anger in Mrs. I.

Mrs. I.: Was I angry at that conference! My husband's
lawyer asked why I don't take the kids. I'm amused,
but I'm angry—angry at him for stirring the pot. I
wonder if maybe I *don't* love the kids. I mean, I enjoy
not being with them. I don't yearn to see them. It
isn't carved in stone that you have to love your kids.
But I *must* love them or I wouldn't have stayed so
close by, and I wouldn't see them so much. I just
can't let them in too close. I've been too hurt. Jenny
wants to be close—she tries.

Therapist: How do you respond?

Mrs. I.: I don't draw away, but I don't move toward her
either. To me, love means pain—to be avoided. I
don't trust any of them. I can't accept the affection.
Jenny made Mother's Day plans. I'd like to back out.

Therapist: It's hard to trust them.

Mrs. I.: It only *looks* good—then the knife goes in. But I want
to love them and I want their love. I'll go along with
their plans. Are you sure it'll be okay—I won't be
hurt?

Therapist: You'd like my assurance. It's so hard to trust them.

In individual therapy, Mrs. I. had an opportunity to explore her own feelings about loving and closeness that had obviously had great impact on her marriage and her relationship with her children. Her desire to maintain the bond with the children was the impetus to self-discovery.

Some months later, Mr. I. went off on a business trip and Mrs. I. agreed to stay with the children in the house for a week. She discovered that the things that had angered her about their attitudes and behavior at home had not changed. However, her reaction was quite different. She realized that in the past her anger had served to distance her from them.

Mrs. I. had become a more loving, caring mother in her non-custodial relationship with her children than she had been when she lived with them. Jenny reportedly improved her school behavior, although she continued to act up occasionally as a means of getting her father's attention. The therapist did suggest that Mr. I., go for counselling, but he refused. At a later date, Jenny went for a brief period of therapy.

A Custodial Mother in Concurrent Treatment with Her Child

Mrs. J. brought her younger daughter, 7-year-old Kim, for evaluation and treatment. The presenting problem was that Kim was immature, whiny, overweight, and hypochondriacal. The pediatrician had suggested therapy. Mrs. J. had been divorced one year earlier and had returned to the community where her parents lived. Mr. J. lived about 250 miles away. Mrs. J. stated that she had come back so that her parents would be available to babysit when she dated. She had taken custody as a matter of course. Neither she nor Mr. J. had considered any other arrangement. However, he had become annoyed when she took the children so far away. Mrs. J. was supported by alimony, child support, and a check from her father's payroll.

Kim was an exceptionally bright youngster who unconsciously wanted to stay a baby. She fantasized being carried and fed. Her hypochondriasis served to get attention and babying. Mrs. J. always referred to Kim as "my baby" and admitted that she had no patience for her 11-year-old daughter, who was showing signs of puberty.

The first therapy session with Mrs. J. revealed several things about her that were crucial to Kim's development.

Mrs. J.: My parents always did everything for me. I never lived on my own. I used to think I was retarded. Even now I have trouble thinking.

Therapist: In what way?

Mrs. J.: Sometimes I say "no" and then "yes" to the kids. I say "no" and then ten minutes later I change my mind. I feel sorry for them. I remember how it was when I was a kid and I'm sorry I'm doing it to them. Bedtime is awful. Last night when I got home, I bathed Kim.

Therapist: You still bathe her. You do to her what you say your parents did to you.

Mrs. J.: But she'll whine if I tell her to do it herself. It's easier to bathe her. I don't mind doing it.

Therapist: You *like* doing things for her.

Mrs. J.: She's my baby.

Therapist: And she plays the part for you. As long as you do things for her that she can do for herself and give her the message that you enjoy it, she'll act like your baby. And some of the babyish behavior, like her whining, bothers you.

Mrs. J. became aware, in therapy, of the ways she had encouraged Kim to be infantile and hypochondriacal.

Mrs. J.: I never loved my husband so I gave to the children. I loved taking care of a little baby. I never left the children alone. But I wasn't really with them either. I'd be on the phone or watching TV. I didn't pay much attention to them.

Therapist: How would they get your attention?

Mrs. J.: Whenever they were sick, I was motherly. I gave them a rubdown. The time Kim broke her collar bone, I was on the phone. I felt terrible. I apologized.

At another session, she saw how food had become an important reward.

Mrs. J.: She started this morning with French toast. I didn't feel like making it. I offered to make it for lunch. Then she refused to get washed. She was hysterical. So I gave her a donut to calm her down.

At about the same point in treatment, Kim played the "Bag of

Words Game" (Gardner, 1976) with her therapist. She drew the word "airplane" and told the following story which revealed how important food was to her.

> Kim: I took an airplane to Florida. On the way down they gave us lunch, and on the way home they gave us dinner.
> Therapist: The meals were important to you.
> Kim: Yeah—it was fun. I like to eat.
> Therapist: What does it feel like when you eat?
> Kim: It feels like my mommy loving me.

The children spent one or two weekends a month with their father. Kim had reported that he was much more "strict" than Mommy. In spite of that, Kim looked forward to the visits. She said she wanted to see her old house and old friends. She seemed to enjoy the thrust toward more mature functioning that her father's expectations and behavior demanded of her. Mrs. J. looked forward to her weekends alone. She acknowledged that she dreaded the return of the children. She began working in therapy on her reluctance to assume responsibility.

Just at this time, Mr. J. suggested that he would like custody of the children. The therapist discussed the proposal with Mrs. J. and with Kim. Mrs. J. saw it as an opportunity to give up responsibility and to avoid coping with her maturing daughters. Kim liked the idea, but was worried that mother would be angry. Mother and daughter were seen together and Mrs. J. was able to assure Kim that she was not angry. Indeed, she wasn't! She was delighted at the prospect. The change was made. Follow-up with Mr. J. six months later indicated that Kim was happy, had not missed a day of school, and had gotten taller but gained no weight.

Mrs. J. was to continue in treatment to work through her dependency needs. However, she met a man some 15 years her senior, married him and had her needs met. She left therapy.

Limitations and Cautions

Benefits to the Children are Indirect

Individual counseling of the parent is only indirectly beneficial to the children. Certainly, it is to the children's advantage to have a mentally healthy, well-adjusted parent. However, unless the child is in concurrent treatment as the referred patient, much of therapeutic time is not likely to be focused on the child's problems or even the parent's problems with childrearing. The children's needs are likely to be incidental to the treatment. The therapist will need to be alert to the children's needs, as in the cases described previously, but the parent is the client.

Problems with Fees

It is important for the therapist or clinic to clearly establish who will be responsible for fees. When a single mother comes for help about the children, the father is frequently, as provider of alimony and/or child support, expected to take care of health care bills. We strongly recommend that the father be contacted and his cooperation be established. Although this will not guarantee that fees will be paid, it does improve the chances. We have seen situations in which the noncustodial father, after treatment has begun, has refused to pay fees. The therapist who is caught in the money conflict between the parents is going to be less effective. It is also recommended that the parent who seeks treatment be held responsible for some portion of the fee, in order to have an investment in the therapeutic process.

Summary

Individual treatment is frequently sought by people who are struggling with the decision to divorce and by people for whom the divorce has created considerable psychological distress. When these patients are also parents, problems with the children will often be the material discussed in the therapy sessions. The therapist has to be aware of the children's needs and to be able to consider them in the light of the needs of the patient/parent. For some therapists, this may mean referring the patient elsewhere to work more educationally than therapeutically with parenting problems.

Sometimes the child is the referred patient or the focus of the parent's reason for seeking help. In these instances, it is easier for the therapist to focus on the child's needs, although again the patient/parent's needs cannot be overlooked. The therapeutic task may be the resolution of the conflicting needs of parent and child.

Individual therapy for a divorced parent allows for dealing with broader issues and conflicts than just those directly involving the children. As the parent grows in other areas, the children benefit from the parent's increased energy, reduced anxiety or depression, ability to function independently, and so forth. Individual therapy is recommended for parents who have obvious psychopathology or symptoms of distress. It is also recommended concurrently for parents of children who are in treatment.

Conclusion

The mental health professional who works with divorced parents has a two-fold task: educational and therapeutic. The modality in which the therapist works will influence the balance between the tasks. A structured parenting group is at the educational end of the continuum and individual therapy at the therapeutic end. The greater the parent's own emotional problems, the less effective the structured group will be and the greater the need for individual treatment because the parent's emotional problems create a barrier to change in the direction of effective parenting.

A group leader needs to be alert to parental pathology and refer a parent for individual treatment when necessary. Conversely, a therapist working with an individual parent may decide to refer the client to a parenting group when parent education appears to be needed.

The therapist who works with a divorced parent advocates two positions, that of the parent and that of the child. The therapist's role is therefore especially sensitive. However, when the client is aware of the dual advocacy, the task can be successfully accomplished.

Chapter 3

The Therapist and the Divorced Parent: When the Child is the Client

When children have emotional problems subsequent to parental divorce, they frequently come to the attention of mental health professionals in schools, in mental health centers, and in private practice. There are a number of ways to intervene therapeutically with these children, including family, individual, and group therapy. The determination of therapeutic modality will depend upon the interaction of several variables. First is the availability of service in the particular system. For example, a school setting may offer only group interventions or a private practitioner may do only individual psychotherapy. Second is the orientation or preference of the professional who is offering the service. Third, the parents may present the child for a particular form of treatment; the child's preference is rarely an issue.

In settings in which several therapeutic modalities are available, the family may rely on the therapist's judgment regarding treatment of choice. The therapist then, in the evaluating process, needs to determine which modality is likely to be most beneficial. A few general guidelines may help the mental health professional make this important decision.

Family therapy often is advisable when the problems in the child seem to arise from continued family conflict or family avoidance of issues. In order to engage in family therapy, the parents' willingness to become involved needs to be assessed as well. Individual therapy can be used when the child manifests his or her problems more intrapsychically then interpersonally. An example is the child who withdraws rather than acts out with other family members. Individual therapy may also be used in situations where the family atmosphere is too highly charged to allow for effective treatment together as a family. Group therapy is preferable when peer issues predominate or when the child is most likely to benefit from modeling of peer discussion of problems.

When the child is the identified client, the therapist necessarily becomes involved with the divorced parent(s) to enlist their cooperation in reaching therapeutic and educational goals. Therapist-parent interaction ranges from direct and complete involvement in a family therapy setting to infrequent or necessary contact due to the therapist's inability to engage uncooperative parents.

Family Therapy

When parents separate, who is in the family? Is the child's family still perceived as mother, father, siblings, and self, or is it now seen as two separate families with the child as a member of each? A psychologist who looks projectively at family drawings of children whose parents have separated will generally see that the family is drawn differently as time passes and the child's perceptions change. The authors have found, in their informal review of several hundred drawings of children from single parent families, that initially the families are drawn intact in spite of the parental separation. The majority of children, within a two-year period following parental separation, draw a family that consists of the child with one parent (usually the custodial) or draw two pictures that denote "the two families." The differences seen in children's drawings with the passage of time suggest that the child gradually accepts the reality of the parental separation and a redefinition of family takes place.

Some children experience much difficulty in redefining their families. Years after the separation, they continue to long for parental reunification or feel in conflict about their loyalty to each parent. The complex nature of the readjustment overwhelms those children who have coping mechanisms that are inadequate for the degree of their trauma; they may need professional help as well as parental support. The process of family therapy provides a way to help children redefine their family and readjust their perceptions.

Family therapy generally refers to the inclusion of family members in a therapeutic process where interactional issues among family members are discussed. In this therapeutic approach, emotional disturbances in individuals are seen as outgrowths of interpersonal conflicts between the family members. Hence, the goal of the family therapy process is the resolution or reduction of pathogenic conflicts and anxiety within the family unit (Rowe, 1975). For a child from a separated or divorced family, the objective of family therapy is to acquire coping skills enabling him or her to disengage from the marital struggle and function in an age-appropriate manner with parents or with other family members who may be hostile or unfriendly towards one another.

When is Family Therapy the Treatment of Choice?

In the situation of marital separation, the child manifests anxieties, frustrations, and other feelings arising from both real and fantasized interactions with each parent or with other members of the nuclear family. Family therapy provides the forum for face-to-face expression and working through of these feelings with concomitant changes in ways of relating to one another. In other cases, the child's aberrant behavior is merely the manifestation of conflicts existing between the parents. As a result of the interpersonal origin of the problems and the interpersonal relationships that sustain or exacerbate these problems, family therapy is often the treatment of choice except in specified situations such as the following: families in which custody is in question; families in which a parent is unavailable for therapy because of abandonment, incarceration, heavy alcohol or drug use; and families in which the danger of retribution exists as in the case of an abusive parent.

Whom to Include

Who is included in the sessions depends upon the conceptual framework used by the therapist and the needs of the family or identified patient. Some family therapists keep all family members together—never seeing them separately, whereas others may advocate separating the family members if this appears judicious. Consideration needs to be given to whether or not to include the noncustodial parent, step-parents, stepsiblings, halfsiblings, other close relatives, or live-in partners. One important criterion upon which the decision can be based is the extent of their involvement in fostering or sustaining the difficulties. A case example shows unresolved conflicts between the natural parents that affect the child, especially at times of scheduled visitations.

> Five years had passed since Bert's parents had separated. The father had left the marital relationship after involvement with another woman who, after the divorce, became his current wife—Bert's step-mother. Bert's mother, on the other hand, had not become reinvolved in a serious relationship, but instead had a number of relationships with whom the prospect of marriage was limited.

Although gifted in intelligence, Bert, now age 9, never did satisfactory school work due to inattentiveness and noncompletion of assignments. He also remained uninvolved with peers and was rejected for his aloofness and unfriendliness. The school psychologist recommended counseling and both parents called the therapist requesting help for their son. Separate sessions were scheduled for the child, each parent, and the stepmother, for evaluation purposes and for determination of the treatment plan.

The mother, as the custodial parent, had been using her son's visitation time to retaliate against her former spouse. Often, when the father was expected to pick up Bert, the mother would have the child with her elsewhere. Depending on how late she returned, Bert's father would either angrily be waiting or would have already left. When packing her son's clothes for a weekend with father, the mother packed clothing inappropriate for the events she knew were scheduled.

The mother also made telephone conversations between father and son uncomfortable by disallowing calls to the father claiming the child was busy when the father called. On occasional permitted calls, the mother stayed near the telephone angrily glaring at the son during his attempted conversation.

The therapist chose to work with different combinations of family members at different times because of the unresolved feelings between the parents making it initially impossible for them to cooperate in their parenting roles.

The therapist saw the natural parents together while seeing the child individually. This was with the knowledge and cooperation of the stepmother who could have sabotaged the treatment had her cooperation not been obtained. Through this approach, the parents released years of pent-up hostility and achieved a greater level of acceptance for the reasons for the marital problems and for their individual coping styles.

The therapist worked with the child alone on his memories and impressions of the divorce and his perceptions of the parental relationship and how it affected him. The child's coping style was explored and use of other methods discussed. After approximately three months of this weekly format, the parents were ready to discuss ways of working together around their child.

The family currently is seen in this format with plans for later inclusion of the stepmother. Communication between family members has improved considerably; there has been greater cooperation in parenting with noticeable changes in the child's ability to relate to his peer group.

Up to this point, the family members have been seen in the combinations mentioned for a total of six months and they are nearing termination of the therapy.

As this case example illustrates, it would have been difficult for the therapist to alter the hostile interactional patterns affecting the child without bringing together the family members. Continued individual therapy with the child alone probably would have brought about changes in the child only. Such a change in the child's level of understanding and ways of coping may have forced changes on the part of the parents. However, there would continue to be pressure on the child to maintain the former interactional pattern since it met the pathological needs of the parents.

A crucial criterion for inclusion of family members is their willingness to become involved in the therapeutic process. In the example above, the involvement of both the custodial and noncustodial parent meant a recognition of the part each of them played in their son's difficulties.

More than half of the noncustodial parents do not, after a one-year period, remain actively involved with their children (Fulton, 1979). The involvement of both parents in the therapeutic process may help promote longer active participation. Goldman and Coane in 1977, particularly advocated inclusion of noncustodial parents as a means of emphasizing the constancy of the parenting roles in spite of the parents' physical separation. They also found that the inclusion of both parents provided an opportunity to correct children's perceptual distortions of the divorce and to help the parents "emotionally" divorce one another. This thinking is in contrast to earlier warnings in the 1960s (Kushner, 1965) that the noncustodial parent should never be seen with the former spouse due to the intensity of emotions which might be expressed. It would appear that the suggestion that the noncustodial parent be included in the therapeutic process was too advanced a notion in 1965 which was prior to much of the recently collected research data on children of separation and divorce.

Active involvement of the step-parents or other parent surrogates is also of importance. Their involvement and support can be instrumental in the willingness of the partner to explore problematic issues. The therapist will need to remain sensitive to the fears and concerns of the step-parent created by the reinvolvement of their spouse with the former spouse. It may be necessary to periodically meet together with the parent and step-parent and encourage their communication regarding the therapeutic process even when one is not directly involved. Step-parents can easily sabotage the therapeutic gains if they feel threatened and uninvolved in the process.

When both parents or step-parents are involved in family therapy, it is recommended that the child not be present initially for several reasons. The process needs to be explained to these other members and accepted by them. They need to understand that they, as parents, are meeting together for the primary benefit of their child. The purpose of the therapeutic sessions is to discuss their child's problems, determine the causes, and plan a united strategy for helping their child. The therapist can help the parents to give priority to their role as parents and to establish a communicative, working relationship which can continue after cessation of the therapy. The therapist than can determine at what point the parents are ready to meet with their child, i.e., when the parents are ready to try to work together as parents rather than against each other as estranged or divorced people. At times, working through their issues as former marital partners has to precede their issues as parents.

Issues to be Addressed

Since individuals define themselves through how others perceive them (Stryker, 1972), children experiencing parental separation undergo a redefinition of the self. They are now perceived by their family members, other adults, friends, and themselves as a "child of divorce" with accompanying stereotypes, prejudices, and feelings. Children can be helped in the self-redefining process during family therapy sessions.

The perceptions parents have of themselves and their necessary redefinitions affect not only their own lives but their children's as well. Pais and White (1979) devised a schematic model of divorce adjustment in which they redefined coparenting roles involving the "rights and duties" of each parent and of the child including custody, child support, and visitation. The dynamics of the parent-child relationship of both the custodial parent and the noncustodial parent are likely to be different from how they were prior to the divorce.

The child, in the process of undergoing a self and family redefinition, may experience emotional detachment from the non-custodial parent or even from both parents. Relationships change, especially those of parents, grandparents, and other relatives. The development of new interpersonal relationships may be necessary, such as with teachers and friends in the event of a move. There may be step-parents and stepsiblings if the parents remarry. In a family therapy modality, children are exposed to the changes in their parents' feelings and values and can be helped in recognizing and understanding their own feelings and values through listening to the parents.

The following lists the major issues that are commonly discussed in family therapy sessions with divorced families:

1. Issues for parents
   - Transition to single parent status
   - Child care responsibilities and discipline of child
   - Dating; remarriage; stepchildren
   - Loneliness
   - Establishing different relationship with former spouse, relatives, and children
   - Financial problems
   - Housing
   - Anger and other unresolved feelings
   - Child-napping
   - Grieving loss of family, spouse, and children
   - Employment
   - Custody decisions and litigation
   - Communication problems
   - Loss of generational boundaries
2. Issues for children
   - Transition to "child of divorce" status
   - Adjustment to visitation schedule
   - Loss of family life and parent
   - Step-parent, stepsiblings, halfsiblings
   - Moving
   - Change of schools, friends
   - Involvement in loyalty issues between parents
   - Involvement in custody issue

In a family therapy modality, children have the opportunity to hear the concerns and views of their parents and to express their concerns and feelings in a supportive family atmosphere. The parents can model the willingness to try to work out problems. They can encourage the development of communication skills. Family members tend to gain a greater appreciation for each other's feelings and a greater respect for their views as they see each other change and grow and as they work together on the process of changing. The child can frequently make therapeutic gains rapidly if he or she receives continuous feedback and if the therapeutic discussions carry over to between-session discussions among the family members.

A child may lack supportive family models or supportive others outside of therapy. Some individual sessions with the child in addition to the family sessions may, in these instances, give the child an opportunity to be alone with the therapist and therein establish a supportive and satisfying relationship. The therapist may, in addition, provide the adult model that was absent or inadequate for a child. A combination individual and family therapy approach may prove beneficial in such circumstances.

Intervention Strategies

Problems unique to divorced families. There are some unique aspects in working with a divorced family of which the therapist should be aware. Within each session, the family therapist is working with individuals who were once an intact family who lived together in the same household, worked and played together, and planned for their futures together. Many crucial changes have occurred including separate residences, traumatic losses, value changes, changes in future plans, and lack of togetherness. The "family" or "families" (depending on how they define themselves), must again learn how to interact with one another, considering that all family members have changed and important circumstances have changed.

The members of the divorced family can explore their altered feelings, values, behaviors, and expectations for themselves and for each other. They can clarify the often gross misunderstandings that occur since the opportunities for communication have significantly lessened. For example, the child often has either a distorted or inadequate understanding of the reasons for the divorce. Or, the child may have been told different ways to act by both parents including what to say or whom to tell. Kelly and Wallerstein (1977) indicate the importance of discovering children's view of the divorce by exploring their understanding of the divorce, what they were told, and their fantasies.

A four-part model. Goldman and Coane (1977) proposed a four-part model for intervention. Their family therapy model included sessions of the divorced parents together with the children. The first step in their conceptual strategy was to help the family members redefine themselves as existentially still a family. The accomplishment of this task attenuated the confusion over the parent's functions and ensuing loyalty conflicts.

Secondly, generational boundaries were firmed, reducing the tendency for children to fill roles left unfilled by parents by ensuring that parents meet their own obligations and responsibilities as parents. The third task was for the family to experience the replay of the marital history, thereby correcting development distortions. Misconceptions tend to occur when the child is young at the time of the event; in the child's wish for reunion, thereby ignoring certain realities; and, through lack of parental contact. New parent-child relationships can be based on reality and adequate information.

The fourth (and what Goldman and Coane describe as the "most difficult task") is to help the parents divorce emotionally. This task is to try to foster the emotional divorce with adults still bonded by their children by helping the parents seek other adult objects and break the cycle of nongratification implicit in their unsuccessful marital relationship. "If accomplished, this has the potential to free the children from being redrawn into the orbit of parentification" (p.362).

Structural family therapy. Kaplan (1977) proposed using the structural family therapy model developed by Salvador Minuchin with divorced families who have symptomatic children. In this model, the therapist works with those subgroups of the family system which may be stressful for the child. The model assumes that the individual is influenced greatly by the social context in which he or she lives and "a change in social context will alter the experience of the individual within it, and the individual will respond with changes in behavior and inner experiences that are adaptive to the changes in the context. Thus, a change in family patterns of interaction—and important social context—will effect changes in the behavior and inner experience of a child within the family" (p.75).

Kaplan has found five family configurations. The first configuration includes the mother, child, and maternal grandparents where the mother, after the separation, either physically returns or turns emotionally to her parents and conflict ensues, particularly affecting the child in the area of conflicts around child raising. The second configuration is the overprotective mother where, in the absence of the father, the overprotected child clings to the mother and the mother focuses even more concern upon the child. The third is the helpless and mildly neglectful mother where the divorce accentuates these characteristics. Fourth is the noncustodial parent (or father in Kaplan's studies) where visitations create conflicts for the child in the areas of loyalty. An example is when the parents use the child as their means to communicate either in an indirect or direct way. (Kaplan suggests meeting with the parents together when possible.) Fifth in Kaplan's model, is the formation of a new family after the dissolution of a previous marriage. Either the children from the former marriage are abandoned or attempts are made to integrate them—both stressful processes. The children can become the focus of disagreement between the new spouses. This last configuration includes couples who divorce and marry new spouses. Kaplan suggests a meeting between both couples when possible in order to remove the child from the focus of disagreement. The therapist's role with the designated family configurations is to deal with current patterns of interaction and relieve the families of interpersonal conflicts in order to provide symptomatic relief for the child.

Limitations and Cautions

Confidentiality. Working with divorced families carries with it additional or, at least, different responsibilities from working with individuals. An example can be seen in the issue of confidentiality. In some states, when working with a family, there is no privileged information between the therapist and clients because the confidentiality laws are modeled after attorney-client privilege which no longer exists when a third party is present. In New Jersey in 1981, a bill was passed specifically extending confidentiality to the group and family therapy situation.

It is important for the therapist to receive clarification on his or her own state laws as well as federal laws pertaining to release of information, confidentiality of records, and other important legal issues.

> The family of Sarah came to the therapist for family therapy in an attempt to try to resolve the serious family issues and avoid the parents separating. The issues were not resolvable in the seven sessions during which the family came. The mother left and took Sarah.
>
> There was no further contact with the therapist until she received a request for information from the probation department that was investigating the case for custody. The request was signed by the father, the noncustodial parent. The therapist contacted the mother who said she did not want the information sent. The therapist contacted her attorney for clarification, who said that the signature of either parent was valid for release of information and advised the therapist to send the requested information.

Such information is also important for institutions such as mental health centers (Drake & Bardon, 1978) and schools (Drake, 1981).

Complexities of blended families. Kaplan (1977) alluded to blended families as one of his conceptualized types of families presenting possible conflict which could be disturbing to a child. Whiteside and Auerbach (1978) delineate common structural subsystems of the remarried family—each parent bringing children from first marriages. The subsystems or potential problem areas include the spouse, stepparents, stepchildren, "ours" children, and relationships with family members outside of the home.

Blended families may come for help with problems within any of the mentioned subsystems. There may be resentment on the part of the spouse for financial responsibilities and other obligations agreed to prior to the union of the reconstituted couple. There might be favoritism or rejection shown toward a certain child. Other examples of problems include conflict in visitation schedules and arrangements, continued or lack of contact with extended family from the previous marriage, or jealousy toward the spouse's relationship with the former spouse.

Avoiding common problems.   It is not recommended that a therapist attempt a family therapy modality without training and supervision. An experienced family therapist will not be likely to fall into some of the possible pitfalls of family therapy. One example that leads to failure of the family therapy modality is the inability of the therapist to engage all of the family members and to establish rapport sufficient for a working alliance with all the family members. The unaligned members attempt to sabotage the participation or growth of the others.

The experienced family therapist tries to avoid collusion with family members. A generally stated rule that avoids collusion is to inform the family members that the therapist will need to feel free to discuss in family sessions what is said privately. This may discourage the parent from disclosing information (such as an extramarital affair), but it also may prevent the therapist from being triangled with one parent. Of course, the therapist will always need to use judgment regarding what information to use and when.

Occasionally, the child tries to make a "couple" of the therapist and a parent (Hajal & Rosenberg, 1978). This may especially hold true when a child of divorce is experiencing the loss of the parent and the therapist is the same sex as the absent parent. The therapist needs to be sensitive to this issue and clarify and interpret for the child the underlying reunion fantasies or fantasies of an intact family consisting of parent and therapist. If this issue is not clarified, there may be an attempt to devalue the therapy because the child feels rejected and unloved.

The Child in Individual Therapy

Many children whose parents are divorced are referred for individual therapy. The particular problems of this group are discussed fully in *Psychotherapy with Children of Divorce* by Richard A. Gardner (1976). Our concern here is the relationship between the child's therapist and the child's parents.

Acclimating the Parent(s)

Before a child begins treatment, it is advisable for the therapist to meet with the parents. Even when the parents are divorced, it is to the child's advantage to have the continued commitment of both parents to the therapeutic process. Both parents need the opportunity to discuss their concerns regarding treatment. Among the most common are their feelings of exclusion, envy of the child's relationship with the therapist, and concern about how the child will change. For some divorced parents, a major issue is the child's relationship with the other parent. They do not want to see an improvement in the relationship, although they may verbalize otherwise.

In acclimating the parents to the therapeutic process, the therapist needs to deal directly with these anxieties so that the parent does not interrupt therapy in order to reduce his or her own anxiety. In addition, the parents should be advised against questioning the child to obtain information about the sessions but rather to allow the information to emerge spontaneously.

Confidentiality

One of the issues with which the child's therapist must grapple is that of confidentiality. The guidelines of confidentiality with a child-client are not clear (McGuire, 1974). Gardner (1976) suggested, that since children below age ten or eleven have little in their lives that is unknown to their parents, their expectations regarding confidentiality are unlike those of adolescents and adults. He considered the advantages of sharing information about the child's treatment with the parents to far outweigh the disadvantages.

A recent study of children's conception of confidentiality (Messenger & McGuire, 1981) revealed that as children get older, they gradually evolve a concept that is consistent with professional guidelines for confidentiality with adults in therapy. As a result, Messenger and McGuire suggested that a graded system of confidentiality be adopted, under which younger children would not be afforded the same degree of confidentiality as older children. This study focused on the sharing of information with the school counselors, but concluded that the access of parents to information about the child also needs to be clarified.

Adolescents, struggling with issues of independence, are especially sensitive to the maintenance of the confidentiality of the therapist-client relationship. When the therapist feels that it is important that a parent be informed in order to be helpful to the child, then the therapist needs to discuss the issue with the child and obtain permission to disclose information. The therapist who reveals information to the parent without the teenager's permission is undermining the trust in the therapeutic relationship.

> Bobby, age 13, was anxious to change his living arrangement, from moving between houses every two weeks, to living with his mother while visiting his father on weekends. He acknowledged to his therapist that he was fearful of his father's reaction to the idea. The therapist offered to speak to the father and pave the way for Bobby's confrontation with him.

> In a session just before he left for two weeks at camp, Bobby said, "I think my father has become deaf. He doesn't listen. I can't stop listening because I'm the kid."

> Therapist: What if I meet with your father, or with both your parents, while you're in camp? We can discuss the change in living arrangements.
>
> Bobby: You can meet with my mother if you want to. Or you can meet with my mother and father together. But if after that, you decide to meet with my father alone, you have to check with me first.
>
> Therapist: I'll do that, but I wonder what you're concerned about.
>
> Bobby: He might get angry.
>
> Therapist: At whom?
>
> Bobby: Me—you. I don't know. Maybe he'd be offended. It's hard to be sure with him.

> It was important to the continuing therapeutic relationship to honor Bobby's instructions. The therapist invited Bobby's parents to come in together, but the father declined. No further overtures were planned until Bobby returned from camp.

In certain cases, it may become essential to inform the parents of behavior or predicted behavior which may prove detrimental to the child. In the areas of potential suicide or homicide, guidelines of the American Psychological Association Code of Ethics should be followed.

There are times when the child-client may become involved in potentially dangerous situations. The therapist needs to exercise judgment regarding the handling of such situations, weighing the risk to the patient versus the risk to the therapeutic relationship if an agreement of confidentiality is made, then broken. When possible, the client can be encouraged to reveal the information to the parents himself.

John, a 14-year-old boy, had come to live with his father and stepmother only two weeks previously. He had been asked to leave the home in which he lived with his mother and younger sister because of continued disobedience.

He had been socializing with newly made friends, one of whom was target-shooting with his Dad's rifle. Bantering between the boys ensued and John was shot in the elbow. John called his therapist from the hospital and told him what happened and who shot him, but did not want his father and stepmother to know for fear of losing his newly-made friends, and because of uncertainty of his stepmother's reactions or acceptance of him. The psychologist did not know the potential for violence of the boy who shot John and knew his parents and the police must be told in order that any further danger to John could be assessed and deterred. The psychologist was able to convince John to tell the truth by discussing the possible ramifications of not telling and discussing his fears regarding his stepmother. The confidential relationship was thus maintained.

Similarly difficult situations include adolescent pregnancy, stealing cars and then driving at high speeds, and drug or alcohol abuse.

Concurrent Treatment of Parent and Child

As indicated earlier, when children or adolescents are referred for individual treatment, it is recommended that a parent be seen in concurrent treatment by the same therapist or by a different therapist. The rationale is that the child can neither change the environment nor leave it. A parent's behavior may be contributing to the child's discomfort. The therapist who sees both child and parent can see the interaction between them, and intervene with the parent on the child's behalf. The parent who enters concurrent treatment does so with the understanding that the child's needs will be a focus of the therapy.

We have found, too often, that when parents are not concurrently involved in their own treatment, they sabotage the child's therapy. They fail to bring the child for appointments or they withdraw the child from treatment at the first sign of improvement. When the child's behavior has supported a parent's neurotic needs or has served a particular function within the family system, a change in that behavior is perceived as a threat to the parent unless the parent's neurosis is also being addressed.

When a parent and child are in concurrent treatment, with the same or different therapists, the confidentiality of the child's communications need not necessarily be broken. There are times when the therapist wants to point out specific incidences of parental behavior, which have been reported by the child and are detrimental. More likely, the therapist and parent will deal with general issues relating to the child and the details will be forthcoming from the parent.

Edward, age 8, complained to his therapist that he hardly ever saw his father. He revealed that his mother seemed just as happy not to have his father visit. Several weeks later, the following occurred in the mother's individual session with the same therapist.

Patient: I don't like their father. I can't stand to see them (Edward and younger brother) going out with him. I kept them away from him too long because I couldn't deal with him. I have to deal with him. I don't see how my feelings can change.

Therapist: You seem to want some change.

Patient: I do. It's not right for the kids. I know Edward wants to see his father. Don't you think so?

Therapist: Yes.

Patient: Then I've got to do something. Anyway, it's not good for me either to be so angry and hold on to it.

Two weeks later, Edward's mother reported, at the outset of a session, that Edward's father had taken him for the weekend. When Edward saw the therapist, he gleefully described the weekend and observed happily that his mother didn't seem to mind at all.

Groups for Children of Divorce

According to a recent study (Kurdek et al., 1981), children adjust better to their parents' divorce when they are able to discuss the situation with their peers. Groups for children of divorce provide an opportunity for sharing and learning. Kurdek et al. (1981) recommended that the groups include a strong cognitive component designed to help children understand and accept their parents' divorce.

Cantor (1977) suggested that schools are an ideal setting for groups for children of divorce for several reasons. First, the children are there. As The Rochester Primary Mental Health Project (Cowen, Trost, Izzo, Lorion, Dorr, & Isaacson, 1975) has indicated, the school is the social institution that, after the family, most profoundly affects human development. Schools are relatively large, geographically bound settings that all people attend. Next, trained personnel are available for group leadership in the school in the persons of school psychologists, social workers, and guidance counselors.

Because there is a reciprocity between the child's psychological and educational problems, the school cannot fulfill its educational function for children who are reacting to the disruption of divorce. For these children, for ten months of the year, the school can provide instant crisis intervention and peer support.

Involvement of Parents

Before beginning the group, the group leader needs to obtain the permission and cooperation of the parents. By offering an educational session to describe the goals and format of the group to parents, the group leader has an opportunity to involve the parents in the process. At that time, the group leader can make it clear that parents may be called or asked to come to conferences if it seems to be in the interest of the child.

In some settings, it is possible to run concurrent groups for divorced parents. Alternately, two institutions can cooperate in offering group programs. For example, a community mental health center can be the setting for a parents' group that parallels a school-based children's group. Consultation between group leaders can ensure that issues raised by the children are dealt with by the parents.

As is the case for children in individual treatment, children in groups often cannot change or improve the situation without the willingness of their parents to change as well. Therefore, it is vital that these parents become involved in the interest of their children.

The Uncooperative Parent

There are times when it is impossible to engage a parent in treatment or even consultation, in spite of the admonition that it is in the child's best interest. The therapist has to decide how to deal with that situation. To refuse to see the child if the parent is unwilling to participate is to deprive the child of any benefit that might accrue from treatment. The therapist who can give up the rescue fantasies and be satisfied to offer the child as much as possible within the context of the individual or group therapy, will not be overly disappointed, even if the child's treatment is prematurely terminated.

The therapist dealing with an uncooperative parent needs also to be aware of his or her own hostility toward the parent so as not to feed the child's anger. Otherwise, the therapist may create the same kind of triangling with the child as occurs when there is hostility between the divorced parents.

There are times when uncooperative parents will respond to environmental structuring. For example, a divorced father who had little to do with his children accepted the responsibility for driving his children to therapy, thus spending time with them and enhancing their view of him. In another instance, where a mother had been refusing to allow the children to visit their father, the beginning of therapy for the children served as a nudge to change her position because she did not wish to appear negatively in the therapist's eyes.

Some parents who profess to be cooperative, nevertheless behave otherwise. They forget the child's appointments, cancel at the first sign of inclement weather, or withhold payment of fees. When this happens, the therapist and parent need to discuss the meaning of the behavior for the parent. The parent who can express the resistance to the child's treatment more directly is less likely to employ passive-aggressive means of expression.

Conclusion

The involvement of divorced parents in the therapeutic process when the child is the client is frequently a difficult task for the therapist. However, when the behavior of the divorced parents is contributing to the child's emotional problems, their cooperation is essential to the child's treatment.

The family therapy modality can prove to be one of the most useful with separated parents because it promotes direct communication and resolution of conflicts around parenting problems. Family therapy is more difficult with divorced than married parents because of the problems involved in defining the family and of the physical separateness of family members. The presence of step-parents further complicates the therapeutic process.

Concurrent treatment for parents of children in individual or group therapy can also prove exceedingly beneficial by reducing parental pathology and by providing a vehicle for communication regarding necessary changes in home environment and in parenting behavior. When a parent enters concurrent treatment, it must be made clear to him or her that the interests of the child will be a major concern of the therapy.

The therapist who is involved with divorced parents when the child is the client, has the task of focusing them on their role as parents, helping them resolve their parenting conflicts, and educating them to be good parents.

Chapter 4

Helping Parents Minimize the Negative Impact of Divorce on Children

If I had been a really good girl, my parents would not have gotten a divorce.
—Amy, age 8

The task of parenting is a difficult one for which most people are unschooled. The difficulty is exacerbated when parents are divorced. They no longer have each other to turn to for help in raising the children, and, the divorce itself creates additional problems that are not present in an intact family.

Concerned parents realize the importance of trying to help their children come through the separation with as few "battle scars" as possible. One of the professional's multiroles in helping a family through the parental separation is the minimization of possible negative effects on children. We strongly advocate a preventive approach, reaching parents early in the separation/divorce process and educating them in general parenting skills and in areas specifically related to divorce and children. However, we know that most parents do not present themselves or their children to mental health professionals until they perceive a crisis or there is chronic discomfort. Then, the educational process may have to wait until crisis intervention or other therapeutic techniques have reduced the florid symptoms.

Helping Parents Communicate
with Their Children
About the Divorce

One way to minimize children's negative reactions to divorce is to help the children understand what is happening around them. Communicating with the children may be difficult for parents who, at this time are typically involved in their own concerns and life readjustments. Helping the children through the separation does not negate the parents' need to attend to their own changes. However, the importance of parental support and intervention for their children at this time cannot be overemphasized.

There are several ways in which parents can learn to communicate with their children, and to support them through their crisis or readjustment period. One approach is to have the parent enlist a therapist's professional opinion about the appropriateness of including the child in some form of therapy—individual, family, or group therapy. An alternate approach is for the parent to work with the therapist toward understanding the child's needs and toward learning skills needed for effectively supporting the child.

When possible, the children need to hear (preferably from the parents), just prior to the separation, of the inevitability of this occurrence and the decisions and plans. Jacobson (1978b), who studied the impact of interparent hostility on the children noted: "If attitudes emerge that lead to facing a situation realistically, rather than those of denial before the event occurs, the chances of developing symptoms can be reduced" (p.177). Children are usually aware that something is wrong in the family and even spy and eavesdrop to try to find out what they need to know. The following example illustrates the dilemma for some children:

> Jerry, an 11-year-old, was chastised by his mother for eavesdropping. In his group counseling session, he discussed his predicament: Neither his mother nor his father told him of impending changes in his life that concerned him. He knew that his mother was considering remarriage but did not know her decision or when the marriage might take place. He knew his father was thinking of moving away but when questioning his father, he was told not to ask questions. His dilemma was to eavesdrop and risk punishment or to live with his anxiety of not knowing about his future.
>
> The children in the group suggested to Jerry that he ask his mother about her plans. The group leader called Jerry's mother in to discuss the impact of her behavior on Jerry and to encourage her to be more open with him.

It is difficult for parents to decide what to tell the children. The principle to be observed by parents is to give sufficient information to clarify confusion and reduce anxiety without overburdening the children with more information than they can handle.

The Parent Who
Does Not Tell Enough

The professional will encounter parents who separate without telling their children. They may accomplish this by saying nothing at all or they may fabricate a plausible story such as, "Dad is going away on a business trip." The rationale for not telling the children or for lying to the children needs to be explored with the parents. They may not wish to open "Pandora's box." They separate, then wait for the children to ask questions. If no questions are forthcoming, they assume that the children are fine and they are relieved of the burden of giving an explanation. But, in reality, the parents' silence may lead the children to understand that this is not a topic to be mentioned.

Some parents think their children are too young to understand. Actually, very young children may not comprehend any verbal explanation other than "Daddy is going bye-bye." Children older than age 3 usually can comprehend at least a simple explanation. It is never too late to provide children with an explanation of the reasons for the separation in language they can understand. As they get older and can better comprehend, they may request or need additional explanations. Some parents assume that they have given their children adequate explanations and are surprised when the children need a repetition of information they had already heard to help them assimilate it at a new level of comprehension.

Parent reticence may be caused by the discomfort that results from the belief that the information must be presented in a strong way, without tears. In reality, the parent's tears and emotional display give the children nonverbal permission to have feelings of their own. The fact that the parent is explaining the separation implies strength in itself.

The Parent Who
Tells Too Much

Overdisclosure is confusing to children. It is not within the bounds of good parenting to give children information which would cause them to turn against the other parent. For example, children do not need to be privy to information about a parent's extramarital affairs or other personal, sensitive matters such as impotence or homosexuality. Unfortunately, situations such as that of Susan are not that uncommon:

> Susan, a 12-year-old child had come to therapy with extreme hostility toward her father and rejection of him. As Susan talked about the divorce, her therapist learned that the mother had

allowed the child to read the information that her lawyer was using in court against her father. Since the child was only exposed to the negative information about the father, the child began to view her father as responsible for the divorce, cruel to her mother during their years of marriage, and a "bad" person.

On the other hand, parents often cannot hide the truth from the children. If the reason for the separation is alcoholism or physical abuse, the children have seen or heard evidence of it and the accuracy of their perceptions needs to be verified.

Thirteen-year-old Jane was referred for therapy after several incidents of acting-out behavior. In the course of treatment, she acknowledged the connection between her behavior and her anger at her divorced mother. Then Jane revealed that she was certain that her mother was to blame in the divorce because she had an affair with Jane's diving coach. Jane's mother had repeatedly denied the affair. Finally, Jane confronted her mother with her anger and her reasons for feeling so certain. Her mother admitted that Jane's perception was accurate. Jane felt relieved, dealt in therapy with her anger at having been lied to, and the acting out ceased.

The older the children, and the more to which they have been privy, the more complete the explanation of the reasons for the separation need to be. Otherwise, the children will become distrustful of the veracity of their parents' statements to them.

Telling the Children

Separating parents often feel overwhelmed and upset. Telling their children about the separation requires an extra expenditure of their energy. One way in which the parents can support each other at this time is to tell the children together. This also communicates to the children that regardless of the fact that their mother and father will not be living together any longer as a family, they will continue to act like parents, interested in the children's well-being. According to research, however, it is most often the mother alone who tells the children (Jacobson, 1978). At the point of impending separation, the parents may be experiencing too much interpersonal conflict to jointly tell their children. Under these circumstances, it is hoped that each parent discusses the separation with the children and states his or her openness to questions.

What Children Need to Know

Parents need to decide how and what to present to the children on the basis of the individual child's needs and maturity. There are some basic guidelines for what information needs to be conveyed to children:

1. The separation is not the child's fault. The parents can tell the children that the separation is due to problems between the two of them. These problems have not been caused by anything the children have done. The younger the children, the more egocentric they are and therefore the more likely to perceive themselves as to blame. The parents' explanation to very young children must consider their perception of their control of what happens around them. Telling them that they are not the cause of the separation will not suffice unless the parents specifically deal with the children's ideas of cause and effect. With older children, having more information about what has really transpired reduces the tendency to take the blame.

   In most cases, the marital separation is caused by the parents' inability to communicate, different interests, sexual problems, financial worries, or general inability to get along with each other. Although the presence of children may exacerbate the problems by adding additional responsibilities or allowing less time alone with each other, it is seldom the case that the children are the cause of the problems between the two adults.

   In special circumstances of which the children are aware, communicating this fact may prove more difficult.

Cecilia, a 13-year-old patient, had been molested by her father for several years. Soon after her disclosure of this information to her mother, the parents separated. It was only within the context of a therapeutic relationship that she was able to realize and accept that her father had emotional problems and his actions, not her eventual disclosure, had caused the separation.

A 34-year-old mother brought her three uncooperative and noncompliant children to therapy for the purpose of facilitating a change in their behavior. During the family sessions, it became clear to the therapist that these were anxious and depressed children who had been repeatedly blamed by the mother for causing the marriage to end, as well as any relationships she had with boyfriends since the end of the marriage. The mother terminated therapy labeling it as "unsuccessful" before she was able to accept responsibility for what happened to her and to stop placing guilt on her children.

2. The children remain loved by *both* parents, that is, even though mother and father no longer love one another and no longer want to live together, the children are still loved. This knowledge soothes the children, reassuring them that the emotional bond they have with both parents remains intact. However, the assurances would be idle words if the parents are unable to develop a mutually satisfying means of insuring the child's emotional connection with both parents (Messinger & Walker, 1981).

   Indeed, there are times when the noncustodial parent does not continue to show caring for the children. In that case it is better to let the children know that while they are still lovable, the absent parent has difficulty being a loving person. To insist that an absent, uninvolved parent still loves the child is to confuse and anger the child.

3. The parents will continue to be involved with their children. When possible, regular visitation with the noncustodial parent should be arranged as well as free access to that parent through notes and telephone calls. If the noncustodial parent lives within walking or bicycling distance, it is helpful for the children to be able to spontaneously visit and interact with that parent. The importance of the child's continued involvement with the noncustodial parent is discussed fully in Chapter 5.

   The parents can demonstrate their continued involvement by making decisions jointly that affect the children. Examples of such decisions would be visitation arrangements and decisions regarding attendance at parent-teacher conferences or school events. If they are unable to discuss and compromise, the parents will need to separately make decisions that affect the children. The decisions may be conflicting and the children will see and capitalize on the discrepancies between the parents' viewpoints.

4. Their lives will change. There are realities which the children will need to know. Some typical changes are: a change in family structure; a change in residence; a mother going to work; less money available for necessities and luxuries; more need for the children to help with chores.

5. There is nothing they can do to change the situation. Some children cannot accept the permanence of the parental separation. They make numerous ineffectual attempts to reunite the

parents. The extent to which some children try to reunite their parents is seen in the example below.

> Vinnie, a 10-year-old child, was seen in a counseling group for children of separation and divorce. For one of the exercises, he drew a picture of a bleeding heart. When explaining the picture, he talked about how hard he had tried to get his parents together again. He explained how good he had been. He said he tried to get them together to celebrate his birthday and the holidays. Initially, he was reinforced in his attempts when his parents temporarily reunited, but since their last separation, all his attempts had met with frustration and he felt upset.

Had Vinnie's parents conveyed directly to him that neither his good nor his bad behavior would change their decision, his manipulative ploys would likely have been less frequent, intense, or durable.

To appease their children, themselves, and/or each other, parents deny the permanence of the separation. If the parents know this is not true, giving false hope only extends the grief and the longing for parental reunification. Some children may experience intensification of confused loyalties. In one case we saw, the child encouraged his father to seek custody of him because he angrily saw his mother as unwilling to "try again" while his father was giving him false hope.

Avoiding the Divorce Triangle

The divorce situation provides an optimum setting in which *triangling* can develop. Triangling can be defined as an involvement of three people in a conflictual situation, usually where the strategy is to join two against one.

In some situations, the parents create the triangle. They use their children to convey information rather than communicating directly with each other. Children used in this way are placed in a position that is detrimental to their well-being. While a few children enjoy access to information that would ordinarily flow between parents, the majority we have seen feel conflicted. This is especially so when they tell a parent information that is upsetting and that results in having to carry back an angry response. In the messenger role children learn too much. They are treated as if they are neutral carriers of information who are in no way a party to it. As messengers, children become overly involved in parental problems. When this happens, there is frequently a diminished investment in school and peers.

While most children are uncomfortable with the messenger role in the triangle, they do not know how to extricate themselves from it. It is the responsibility of the parents to undo the triangle by communicating directly with each other. A therapist may find it necessary to bring together a long divorced couple in order to work with them to break the triangle.

In some divorced families, the children create the triangle. For example, they may threaten to live with the other parent. Children can sense how upsetting this is to a separated parent, especially one afraid of losing custody. In fear of the child's power to carry through on this threat, the parent gives in to the child's demands. The parents can undo this kind of postdivorce triangle by making it clear that the child cannot manipulate the custody situation at will.

Allowing Children to Express Feelings

Children who can express their feelings openly are more likely than unexpressive children to develop coping skills to help them with family interactional problems.

Many parents need help in allowing their children the expression of sadness, anger, and grief. Few parents will tell their children to stop smiling, but telling children to stop crying is common. Parents can be taught to reflect feelings, for example, responding to a crying child with: "You seem upset today." Parents have even been trained in the filial therapy model to be their children's therapists (Guerney, 1964). Arnold (1978) noted that, at another level, "an effective parent is the child's most important therapist" (p.6). Indeed, parents who are sensitive to their children's emotions and respond supportively, can reduce the children's emotional turmoil and increase their level of emotional maturity.

It is difficult for some parents to respond empathically to their children because of their own problems in coping with feelings. The children's expression of feelings such as sadness or anger makes parents feel what they are trying to suppress.

In order to help parents help their children, we have found three approaches which the therapist can use:

1. The therapist can explore the parents' feelings and explore various coping skills. The parent then feels better prepared to cope with the feelings of the children;
2. The therapist may educate the parent regarding how to approach the child, teaching the parent to clarify, reflect, or empathize;
3. A family therapy approach can be used where the parent(s) and children are seen together. By working with the family

members as a group, the mental health professional can watch their interaction, understand the children's needs and help the parent respond to those needs.

Sometimes parents find it easier to discuss feelings with their children if they can retain a little distance. Reading books about divorce situations with the children can provide a safe vehicle for such discussions. (See Appendix B).

Keeping Interparental Hostility in Check

The way in which parents conduct their postdivorce relationship has a significant effect on the children. When one parent speaks to the children about the other parent, it is important that the words and the manner in which they are expressed demonstrate respect for the children's feelings about the other parent. The majority of children, even in extreme situations of abuse and neglect, continue to maintain positive feelings about their absent parents and wish for contact. The one situation in which the authors have found this not to be the case is when one of the parents has very negative feelings toward the former spouse and the child is drawn into siding with that parent against the other. It is detrimental to the child to be thus deprived of a relationship with a parent. A case example of the transmission of negative feelings from parent to child and the effect on the child follows:

> Jack, a ten-year-old extremely bright child, was brought to the therapist for help with his antisocial, oppositional behavior. He refused to comply with his parents wishes, calling them names, throwing objects at them, and doing the opposite of what they would request of him. For example, he would turn the radio up when they asked to have it turned down. The mother had less difficulty because she made fewer requests of the child and set fewer limits on him.
>
> The child's behavior reached proportions felt to be dangerous to others, and hospitalization was recommended. Within a few days, the mother and child left the father, because the mother held the father responsible for Jack's behavior calling the father "too strict." The father continued to try to maintain contact with his son but the boy refused gifts sent. He made collect telephone calls to the father only to curse at him and tell him of his hatred for him. The mother encouraged Jack's behavior, and even gave him information to support his anger toward his father. Jack, out of

loyalty to his mother, refused any positive contact with his father. His antisocial behavior increased.

It is commonplace that around the time of separation and divorce, couples regard each other with negative feelings and argue, criticize, and blame each other. Hetherington (1977) found that 66% of the interchanges between divorced couples in the two month period following their divorce were conflictual. Gardner (1978) explains some of the hostility analytically:

> . . . one of the contributing factors to the severely hostile interaction that is so characteristic of many divorces is the reaction formation element, viz., some of the anger serves to deny and repress unacceptable loving feelings that are still present and press for eruption into conscious awareness. (pp. 242–243).

However, the couple, for the sake of the children, need to deal with their difficulties privately, neither being actively abusive in front of the children nor passively criticizing the parent who is not present. When parents expose the child to the hostility between them, the child may develop emotional problems.

> Mr. F. brought his 8-year-old daughter to therapy. On the surface the child seemed to be well adjusted with friends and had good school grades. The father surmised from the scratches on the child's arms and from the behavior of the family cat that Jennifer was abusing the animal. As the therapy progressed, Jennifer spoke about numerous loud arguments between the parents where the police became involved. She spoke of her mother's unwillingness to cooperate regarding bringing her home after visitation, and not allowing her to take home her glasses and school books after one visitation. She reported that her mother was inflexible regarding times of visitation even if that meant Jennifer was unable to do something special she had planned.

> During the therapeutic process, Jennifer disclosed she had been beating the cat when frustrated by her parents' arguments. The behavior stopped as she was able to more openly discuss her situation and feelings, and as her father made a concerted effort to avoid fighting with his former wife in his daughter's presence.

Wallerstein and Kelly (1974) noted that one factor associated with disturbance in adolescence was continued unabated turmoil between parents during the separation. Jacobson (1978a) found that ". . . an important aspect of a child's adjustment to the life event of parental separation is the amount of interparent hostility to which the children have been exposed" (p.17). Parental display of animosity toward one another upsets children, diluting their capacity to cope with their feelings and the significant changes in their lives.

This does not mean that children cannot hear realistic information that may be negative about the other parent, but how this information is presented needs to be considered.

> Mrs. G. brought her bright, 6-year-old son to therapy for his disobedience and encopresis. The father had moved to a distant state after the separation and had infrequent contact with his son. When in the area, he sometimes did not see his son and the child would find out from playmates that his dad had been seen in the area.
>
> When visiting his son, the father would make promises to send gifts that would never arrive. The father was late for visitations or did not come. The mother reported to the therapist that she made angry resentful comments about the father, berating him to the child by calling him "that no good father of yours."
>
> Mrs. G. and her therapist talked about the importance of responding sensitively to her son's pain. She needed to separate her own anger at her former husband from her son's feelings. Then she was able to discuss the boy's feelings with him and to explain to the child that his father did not always keep his word and she did not understand it, but it was something they both needed to accept. Both acknowledged that they could not expect daddy to follow through on his promises. In these talks, the child found the mother to be supportive of him and the disappointment of this father's neglect was accepted more easily.

Encouraging Visitation

The subject of visitation is addressed more fully in Chapter 6, but it also needs to be mentioned here as an important way to minimize childrens' negative reactions to divorce. Children who have frequent contact with the noncustodial parent experience less of a loss as a result of the divorce than do children who are deprived of the contact.

Visitation can have an impact on a child's self-esteem. In our observations, a child's self-esteem is temporarily endangered when parents separate. One study investigating boys who saw their absent-from-the-home parent once a month or more, found their self-esteem to be significantly higher than the self-esteem of those boys who saw their noncustodial parent less than once a month (Lowenstein & Koopman, 1978). Adolescent girls who had little contact with their absent fathers demonstrated inappropriate interactions with males, seeking inordinate attention and becoming involved in heterosexual behavior at an early age (Hetherington, 1977).

Parents, recognizing these as other potential problem areas, can work together by separating visitation from other issues. For example, a common response of custodial parents who do not receive regular child support payments is to deny visitation privileges to the noncustodial parent. Conversely, noncustodial parents who are not allowed to see the child as often as they would like, frequently withhold support payments. A therapist working with members of a divorced family may find this a crucial issue around which to bring the parents together to work toward a solution.

Parents often make each other uncomfortable by threatening to take the child, not return the child, not allow the parent to see the child, and so on. Having the child ready for the parental visit on time and returning the child on time or calling when lateness is unavoidable alleviates the parent's anxiety and leads to a reduction of fear that the child will be used as a weapon against the other parent. When one parent finds the other parent using the child as a weapon, the parent can try to point out to the other parent the potential harmful ramifications to the child and to their relationship as parents to this child. The parent can also talk to the child about his or her feelings regarding being used in this way, and about ways to prevent it. The child with one parent's permission can refuse to be a party to the other parent's game.

Fostering Sameness

Hodges et al. (1979), reported that it is not the divorce event itself but the cumulative stress that negatively affects a child's emotional well-being. As a result, when such a significant and upsetting change as parental separation occurs in a child's life, it is reassuring to have other aspects of their lives remain the same. Therefore, whenever possible after separation, the children should continue to live in the same house or apartment, attend the same school, have the same playmates, and see the same relatives. To some parents, a marital separation means separating themselves not only from their spouse but also from relatives of their spouse. The children would benefit in most circumstances from continuing to spend time with grandparents, aunts, uncles, and cousins. These relatives may provide support to the parents as well as to the children.

Securing Additional Help

If the above ways of minimizing problems prove insufficient, parents may need to secure professional consultation regarding their children. Therapeutic intervention may be advisable. To determine whether a child needs therapy, the mental health professional can discuss with the parent such indices as the degree and extent of the problem, length of time the symptoms have persisted, and the type or nature of the problem. It is important to ascertain how the child functions in school, in the neighborhood, and at home. From the longitudinal studies of children of divorce (Wallerstein & Kelly, 1980; Kurdek et al., 1981), we know to expect some mild symptoms for a period of six months to a year (see Chapter 1). Symptoms that persist beyond that period may require therapeutic intervention. Severe symptoms, such as anorexia, encopresis, and mutism require immediate attention. Finally, disturbances that are apparent in school or with peers are frequently more serious than the lack of cooperation, sibling rivalry, or angry outbursts at home. If therapy is indicated, the parent can be directed to a community mental health center or to a private practitioner. If a different school setting seems advisable, or if additional help in school is needed, the parent can be directed to special services personnel in school or to the child's guidance counselor.

Cantor (1977) has recommended that groups for children of divorce be established within school settings to provide peer support and professional guidance for youngsters and to help avert later serious personality disorders. Schools are suggested as the site for the groups because that is where the children are, and because schools cannot fulfill their educational function for children who are undergoing emotional distress in response to divorce. Groups can be led in schools by school psychologists, social workers, or guidance counselors.

The Role of Other Professionals

Encouraging Parental Contact with Schools

Drake (1981a)) reported a circular phenomenon that has reduced the information available to the schools. Parents have been reluctant to give information about their separation to the schools for fear their children will be stigmatized; schools have been reluctant to seek personal information which may be useful in supporting children through this transition in their lives. Parents sometimes need encouragement to provide the schools with information. They can be helped to perceive the teacher as someone who can be helpful to the child during this time (Gardner, 1978). An informed teacher may boost the child's self-esteem or provide additional academic support when needed. Examples of useful information for the teacher to have include: times during which the home atmosphere is particularly stressful and may carry over into school performance or behavior; and absence of one parent (in order that parental surrogates may be supplied).

When possible, the inclusion of both parents in the child's school activities is encouraged. This may mean sending duplicate report cards or duplicate notices to the residences of both parents. It may mean the alternate attendance by the parents at important activities or an agreement regarding which parent (or both if the relationship is amicable) attends which event. We encourage the mental health professional to work with the parents in understanding the importance of the continued involvement of both parents in all aspects of the child's life.

In addition, mental health professionals can train school personnel to recognize when children of divorce are under duress and to intervene effectively (Drake, 1979). School personnel can become effective supports by offering attention, sympathy, and tolerance as well as providing a stable figure in the environment.

Securing the Cooperation of the Legal Profession

Frequently, lawyers are the first professionals with whom parents establish contact as they contemplate separation and divorce. Lawyers traditionally take an adversary position, which means that they see themselves as having to advocate the client's position. In a divorce, the children typically do not have an attorney representing them, unless a *guardian ad litem*[1] is appointed when the case goes to court.

Mental health professionals who understand the impact of divorce should take the responsibility for educating the lawyers in their communities. There are several suggestions that can be made to lawyers that can serve to help the children. Since lawyers see the parents first, they can remind their clients to focus on the children's needs from the outset. Most attorneys feel they are not equipped to deal with the emotional ramifications of their clients' situations. Attorneys who are knowledgeable about mental health realize their limitations and are more likely to advise their clients to seek the services of mental health professionals.

One of the authors addressed the local bar association about the impact of divorce and custody arrangements on children. Several

---

[1]*Guaradian ad litem* is one who is appointed by the Court to protect the interests of a minor child in a lawsuit. He or she is empowered to act in the child's behalf until the case is concluded.

weeks later, a lawyer who had been in the audience called, wondering whether it would be appropriate to refer a client whom he had just seen for the first time. He described the client as very upset by the separation and having particular difficulty dealing with her two adolescent sons. The attorney revealed that, prior to hearing the author's talk, he would not have thought to help his client in this way.

Attorneys can question their client's motives for seeking custody, and discourage any parent from seeking custody for reasons of vengeance, a power struggle, or as a bargaining device. It is helpful to present the following situation to attorneys: "Suppose a custody evaluation which you have sought shows your client to be the less suitable parent? Could you try to convince your client not to seek custody and in that way continue to advocate your client's position, while at the same time being a child advocate?"

Similarly, attorneys who are aware that visitation is not the real issue, but is rather a vehicle for parents to express hostility, may be able to discourage clients from unnecessarily involving the children in the battle. They and the judges are also in a position to clarify to children who are interviewed in custody proceedings that their statements will not be the determining factor.

It has been the authors' experience that the legal community is receptive to the ideas that have been presented, and will use them to the advantage of children of divorce. Mental health professionals are urged to take the responsibility for clarifying these issues to their legal colleagues.

Conclusion

A marital separation constitutes a very difficult adjustment period for those involved—adults and children. However, parents, as adults, have developed coping mechanisms to lessen the effects of stressful situations. Adults can call their friends, seek professional help, and join supportive organizations. They have the vocabulary to express their anger and pain. Children, on the other hand, often are instructed not to mention the separation to anyone. They do not or cannot seek out help if needed. They often do not have the coping mechanisms to satisfactorily release the anxiety, frustration, anger, and pain or to alter their lives in such a way that gives them strength.

As a result, it becomes crucial for parents to help their children through the crisis and its ramifications, and it becomes crucial for therapists or other mental health professionals to help the parents do so. Jacobson (1978b) stated that ". . . whether or not parents are able to become meaningfully involved with the needs of their children at this time is related to how they themselves emotionally cope with the separation" (p.190). One focus of the professional can be on increasing the coping skills of the parent. But, the therapist cannot neglect the "parent portion" of the adult and needs to look for ways to help the child.

The impact of divorce is minimized for the child who is aware of what is happening, who is permitted to express feelings, who is not caught in a postdivorce triangle, whose schooling and friendships are unchanged, who has access to the absent parent, who does not experience ongoing parental hostility, and who is taught any necessary coping skills. The mental health professional's goal in working with divorced parents is to accomplish as many of these as possible.

Chapter 5

Helping Parents
Decide on
Custody Arrangements

How can a judge decide which of my parents I
should live with? He hardly knows me or them.
I think the family should decide.
—Peter, age 11

Having custody means having possession, power, authority, and responsibility for one's children. Divorcing parents must reach a decision regarding custody and most of them do so out of court. It is estimated that fewer than 10% of custody decisions are made in court (Weiss, 1979). However, the influence of the judge extends to the lawyer's offices, where a pretrial decision may well be based on the anticipation of what the judge's decision would be. Historically, there have been periods in which different custodial arrangements have been favored by the courts.

Custody: a Historical Perspective

England

At the present time, with fathers trying to break the pattern of preference for maternal custody, we may lose sight of how short the history of that preference has been. Historically, fathers had the earliest rights to custody of their children. In eighteenth century England, the father's right, as head of the household, was almost without limit (Derdeyn, 1976b). English law was based on the precedent of Roman law, that had given the father absolute control over his children. Roman fathers could sell or condemn their children to death. During the Middle Ages, children in England were viewed much as servants by the courts, with their rights in the hands of the Manor lord/father. Thus, common law gave custody to the father unless he was proven unfit (Schwitzgebel & Schwitzgebel, 1980). Mothers had no power over their children.

During the nineteenth century, people began to perceive children differently. Society recognized that they needed special care. With that recognition, the role and status of the mother changed, being seen as increasingly important to the child's development (Roman & Haddad, 1978). The English courts assumed jurisdiction over the welfare of children. One of the first men to lose custody of his children was Percy Bysshe Shelley. In 1817, his children were taken from him because of his atheistic beliefs (Derdeyn, 1976b).

In 1839, Talfourds Act gave substance to the court's power to determine custody for children under age 7, under the doctrine of "parens patriae" that held that the Crown should protect all those who have no other protection (Derdeyn, 1976b). (In the United States "parens patriae" refers to "the State, as a sovereign—referring to the Sovereign power of guardianship over persons under disability; such as minors, and insane and incompetent persons." Schwitzgebel & Schwitzgebel, 1980, p.300).

Increasingly, mothers were given consideration in custody through a series of acts, culminating with the Guardianship of Infants Act of 1925, that declared fathers and mothers equals with respect to custody of their children (Derdeyn, 1976b).

United States

Custody in the United States in the early 1800s clearly reflected American law's roots in English common law. Fathers were seen as having superior rights to custody. In Rhode Island in 1824, Justice Story was called upon to decide on custody between a father and a grandfather. His decision questioned the notion of the father's absolute vested right, although the right was upheld. Story introduced the concept of the child's interest, referring to the benefit of the infant, his nurture, care, maintenance, and education (Derdeyn, 1976b; Roman & Haddad, 1978). Increasingly, during the nineteenth century, custody decisions referred to the child's interests. In 1839, a 21-month-old girl was given to her mother, but at age 4, she was returned to her father's custody. In 1857, a New York judge did consider a 6-month-old child's tender years and need to be at the mother's breasts. Nevertheless, after reviewing the evidence, he awarded the child to the father. In 1881, an Arkansas case referred to the father's superior ability to provide financial support as the basis for awarding custody to him. Some courts, during that period, even absolved the father of the responsibility of supporting his child if he did not have custody (Derdeyn, 1976b). It was not until the early 1900s that statutes and case law changed that concept and required noncustodial fathers to support their children. At that point, a major stumbling block to maternal custody was removed. It has been suggested that the child labor laws had an unexpected effect on custody considerations. As children became an economic liability because they were prohibited from working, fathers were less inclined to want custody.

As the United States became more industrialized and men worked away from the family, the mother's role in raising the children became paramount and maternal care was recognized as vital to children. At the same time, women were becoming more independent. They achieved the right to own property and to vote. Gradually, they were given the right to custody, based on the doctrine of "tender years." Initially, "tender years" meant up to age 2½ or 3; but it was extended by court precedent up to adolescence.

Although the "tender years doctrine" was not made into law, it did become one of two major bases of determination of custody. The other was the notion of the best interest of the child, that appears in the statutes of 48 states. With these two principles, the mother developed superior rights to custody, beginning in the 1920s. In the 1960s, it was estimated that mothers were given custody in 90% of cases (Derdeyn, 1976b).

The phrase "best interest of the child" is very vague and presents few legal guidelines. In an effort to clarify the phrase, the Michigan legislature established standards for the courts to employ:

1. The love, affection, and other emotional ties existing between the competing parties and the child.
2. The capacity and disposition of competing parties to give the child love, affection, and guidance and continuation of educating and raising of the child in its religion or creed, if any.
3. The capacity and disposition of competing parties to provide the child with food, clothing, medical care, or other remedial care recognized and permitted under the laws of this state in lieu of medical care and other material needs.
4. The length of time the child has lived in a stable, satisfactory environment and the desirability of maintaining continuity.
5. The permanence, as a family unit, of the existing or proposed custodial home.
6. The moral fitness of the competing parties.
7. The mental and physical health of the competing parties.
8. The home, school, and community records of the child.
9. The reasonable preference of the child, if the court deems the child to be of sufficient age to express preference.
10. Any other factor considered by the court to be relevant to a particular child custody dispute.

(Schwitzgebel & Schwitzgebel, 1980)

In other states the phrase has retained its vagueness allowing for wide variation in its interpretation.

Lowery (1981) surveyed the circuit court judges and commissioners in the state of Kentucky to determine what factors they considered in making custody decisions. The judges, according to their self-report, attach greater importance to their assessment of each parent as a mature, responsible adult and to the wishes of the child and professional advice than to the continuity and diversity of social relationships in the custodial home. Lowery concluded that there are discrepancies between the judges' opinions and the implications of recent psychological research.

Recent Developments

In the decade of the 1970s, the needs of the child became the focal issue in making custody decisions. In 1971, a Missouri court recommended that the tender years presumption be discarded as an outdated stereotype and be replaced by a more realistic appraisal of the needs of the child (Derdeyn, 1976b). In a 1977 New Jersey decision, a judge ruled that the consideration of the tender years theory must always be considered subordinate to what is truly in the child's best interest (Superior Court of New Jersey, 1977). There has been a movement away from considering which parent is at fault in the divorce as a factor in awarding custody, since it is recognized that causing the break-up of the marriage may not be relevant to the issue of being an adequate parent. Automatic favoring of one sex parent over the other is being perceived as sexually discriminating, in keeping with the social trend toward sexual equality.

In 1973, *Beyond the Best Interest of the Child* (Goldstein, Freud, and Solnit, 1973) was published, creating interest and internal debate among members of the legal and mental health professions. Goldstein, Freud and Solnit proposed that the best guideline for child placement is "the least detrimental available alternative for safeguarding the child's growth and development." (Goldstein et al., p.53). The least detrimental alternative, according to them, depends on the maintenance of a continuous relationship with the adult who is or will be the psychological parent. One becomes the psychological parent by being present and active in the care of the child. Goldstein, Freud and Solnit recommended that each child placement be final and unconditional, in order to ensure the relationship with the psychological parent. They went so far as to say that "noncustodial parents should have no legally enforceable right to visit the child, and the custodial parent should have the right to decide whether it is desirable for the child to have such visits" (p.38).

The Goldstein, Freud and Solnit position is not supported by more recent research. Jacobson (1978c), in a study of 30 families, found that the more time lost with the absent parent, the higher the maladjustment of the child in the 12 months following separation. Wallerstein and Kelly (1980) reported that their studies supported a view diametrically opposed to that espoused in *Beyond the Best Interest of the Child.* The results of their research indicated that a relationship with both parents is desirable for the emotional well-being of the child. Consequently, they recommended that wherever possible the postdivorce arrangements permit and foster children's relationships with both parents.

One of the newest custodial plans that complies with Wallerstein and Kelly's recommendation is that of joint custody (Grote & Weinstein, 1977; Roman & Haddad, 1978) or co-parenting (Galper, 1978). In these arrangements, the responsibility of child rearing continues to reside in both parents, although the formula for meeting the responsibility may vary infinitely, depending on the talents, values, needs, and resources of each family. Neither parent is banished and neither parent is overburdened (Roman & Haddad, 1978).

Because domestic relations law is an area reserved to the states by the 10th Amendment to the Constitution, laws affecting custody vary from state to state. The American Bar Association has proposed a Uniform Divorce and Custody Act that directs judges making custody decisions to consider the wishes of the child and both parents, the child's adjustment to home, school, and community, and the mental and physical health of all of the parties (Weiss, 1979). It forbids the judge to consider conduct of a parent that does not affect the parent's relationship to the child (Schwitzgebel & Schwitzgebel, 1980).

Forty-six states (Congressional Research Service, Library of Congress, October 1981) have passed the Uniform Child Custody Jurisdiction Act. (As of October 1981, only Massachusetts, Mississippi, and South Dakota had not passed it and Texas has an equivalent statute.) The law makes custody decisions of one state binding in others. It is intended to diminish the practice of taking a child to another state and beginning a new custody suit.

Helping Parents Arrive at a Custody Decision

Influence of the Therapist's Own Values

Some years ago, at a professional interview, one of the authors was presented with some case material involving a mother and her teenage daughter and then queried, "In view of the fact that you are a mother, what would you tell *this* mother to do?" The reply was, "I would hope that in this case, as with any other patients that I see, my own status and values would have no influence on my recommendation to the mother. What *is* important is what would be best for the individuals involved."

As mental health professionals, it is imperative that we separate our own values from what is best for our clients. When custody is at issue, this becomes exceedingly important. The professional who views one model of custody as the sole acceptable model is unable to meet the client's needs, whether the client is perceived as the child or as one of the parents. The professional needs to be open to the advantages and disadvantages of various models for custody and to be prepared to objectively evaluate the circumstances in each case on their own merit. Among the factors to be considered are the relationships between the child and each parent, the ability of the parents to separate their parenting role from their marital roles, and the maintenance of environmental stability.

On the other hand, it would seem that there is one value that is important for the professional to possess in helping parents reach custody decisions: namely, what is best for the child supersedes all other considerations. In custody matters, it is helpful for the professional to be a child advocate. Every effort should be made to be influential in minimizing the ill effects of the divorce process on the children. Gardner (1976) stated that custody litigation is by far the most vicious and venomous form of marital litigation. Weiss (1979a) called it "the closest thing to a holy war" in the modern world. We agree with Gardner's conclusion that mental health professionals and lawyers should strongly encourage divorcing couples to arrive at their custody arrangements without resorting to litigation. In June 1981, a special committee of the New Jersey Supreme Court, in a report on matrimonial law, recommended that the adversarial approach to custody cases be reduced for the sake of the children.

Custody litigation is frequently muddled by issues other than a parent's sincere desire to raise the children. Parents use custody battles as an arena in which to vent their hostility at the former spouse. The object of winning the battle is the victory over the ex-partner rather than the child's well-being. Mental health professionals cannot succumb naively to the belief that every parent who insists on custody wants it for appropriate reasons, and must be alert to and prepared to expose hostile, devious motives.

In other cases, attorneys have recommended that their clients sue for custody and then use it as a bargaining device. The notion is that the parent will drop the suit in return for a concession by the other parent, such as a reduction in alimony or child support. In these cases, the children are being used as pawns in the game of divorce. The stakes are too high for mental health or legal professionals to be party to the game.

Extricating the Children from
the Custody Process

> Peter, age 11, was seen by a psychologist as part of a custody
> evaluation. He said that he loved both his parents equally. If
> asked to choose between them he wouldn't know what to do.
>
> "If I say I want to live with my mother, my father will think I don't
> love him, and vice versa," he explained.

Peter verbalized the feelings of the majority of children, who want to
be with both parents. However, when a custody decision is made in
court, children sometimes feel pressed to make a choice. They may be
interviewed by an agent of the court, generally from the Probation
Department. It is important that the interviewer and the parents let the
children know that although their views are being considered, they
will not determine the court's decision. Not only is that the truth, it
alleviates a great deal of anxiety and guilt for the child.

> Mr. and Mrs. B. were involved in a custody battle. Thirteen-year-
> old Margie, their oldest daughter, woke up nightly, unable to
> breathe. Her mother brought her for therapy.
>
> Margie discovered that she awoke in fear as a result of the
> enormous pressure that her father had placed on her. He had told
> her that the judge would ask her which parent she chose to live
> with, and that because she was the oldest child, the judge would
> honor her wishes. Margie wanted to live with her mother, but
> was frightened that if she verbalized that desire and her mother
> did win custody, her father would blame her and behave violent-
> ly toward her.
>
> When Margie learned from her therapist that her word was only a
> small part of the basis of the judge's decision, she was able to
> sleep without disturbance.

If the child is the client, he or she can be told directly, as Margie was. If
the parent is the client, he or she has to be helped to understand the
burden that is being placed on the child and to be encouraged neither
to directly state nor to project the expectation that the child will choose
him or her.

Custody to Mother

In the 1980s, although there will be a move toward other custody
arrangements, it is likely that mothers will continue to assume custody
in the majority of divorcing families. Although more fathers are aware

of their equal rights, the number assuming custody has not grown significantly in the past 15 years. Meanwhile, between 1960 and 1978, the proportion of children in the United States living with the mother only more than doubled from 8.2% to 17.6% (Bureau of the Census, 1979).

The concept that it is "normal" for mother to have custody makes it difficult for mothers who do not want custody of their children or feel it would be in the child's best interest to have a custodial father.

> Mrs. C. sought individual therapy as she struggled with the decision to leave home. She and her husband agreed that their marriage was unstable. Mrs. C. was unhappy with her role as wife and mother. She was conscious of wanting to get out of the house and establish herself as an individual, with a career. She wanted little financial assistance from Mr. C. In spite of all her apparent self-awareness, it took nearly a year for Mrs. C. to move out.

> First, she had to deal with her own guilt, stemming from her belief that a good mother would never leave her children. Although she intended to live nearby and remain in constant touch with her teenagers, she was overcome with guilt. Then, she had to work the decision through with her children, particularly a 12-year-old son who reinforced her guilty feelings. To have made the move prior to the resolution would have been psychologically damaging to mother and son.

Mental health professionals are likely to meet custodial mothers after the decision has been reached and implemented, when the stress of functioning as a single parent has become overwhelming. When that happens, the children are likely to be feeling the impact of mother's depression, hostility, anxiety, feelings of inadequacy, or some combination of these. It is for this reason, that preventive approaches are so desirable. If single mothers can be reached and helped before they are overwhelmed, the likelihood is that the cumulative stress for the children will be greatly reduced.

Custody to Father

It is ironic that although custody was historically implicitly the father's, the trend made such a complete reversal after the 1920s that fathers in the 1980s are only beginning to be perceived as equal to mothers as potential custodial parents. The Academy Award-winning film *Kramer vs. Kramer* did much to normalize the image of the custodial father and to portray him as reasonably competent and capable of nurturing even a young child. The film elicited the empathy of the viewer toward the father's right to custody. Nevertheless, the trend toward paternal custody is slight and is presently a predominantly white middle-class phenomenon (Lowery, 1981). In the period 1960–1978, the percentage of children under 18 living with their father only rose from 1.2% to 1.6%, while the number of children living with mother more than doubled (Bureau of the Census, 1979).

When custody is an issue (although mothers and fathers enter the court technically equal before the law), the burden of proof still rests with the father. Molinoff (1977) advised fathers who sincerely wanted custody to be totally committed to the goal; to be prepared to spend a great deal of money; to employ an attorney who is an expert at matrimonial law and who believes in paternal or joint custody, and to refuse to leave the house so that there is no chance of being charged with abandonment of the children.

> The father of a 1-year-old girl sought advice from a therapist. His wife had had a breakdown subsequent to the child's birth, had been hospitalized for four months, and had been diagnosed as "schizophrenic, chronic undifferentiated type." During the hospitalization, the father learned that his wife had had several previous hospitalizations. He decided to seek an annulment of the marriage. His questions for the therapist concerned the genetic nature of schizophrenia and the advisability of seeking custody of his daughter. The lawyer whom he had retained had, according to the client, advised him not to bother seeking custody because, as a father of such a young child, he didn't stand a chance of winning despite his wife's condition. The therapist recommended that he find a lawyer who would take his position and not be prejudiced against paternal custody. The therapist did not suggest that the father should or would get custody of the child, since the therapist had not evaluated him or his wife for custody. Rather, if he felt that he was the better parent, he should take the necessary steps to pursue custody.

Salk (1977), himself a custodial father, recommended that we abandon the negative approach in which a parent is proven unfit and replace it with a positive approach in which both parents are assumed to be fit, but one is better able to meet the needs of the child. This recommendation is consistent with the less punitive and accusatory approach to divorce through no-fault divorce.

Fathers who decide to seek custody need professional help in a number of areas. They may want to evaluate their motives for seeking custody. If they have been equal partners in the raising of the children, as is more frequently the case today when both parents are employed, then their motive is more likely the same as that of a mother: they do not want to be separated from their children. They want to continue to be actively involved in the childrearing. Lamb (1979) predicted that these men would be successful parents because they are a highly motivated and selected group. Fathers who have not shared the responsibility for childrearing need to sort out their anger at their wives from their desire to be sole parent to the children. Gersick (1979) claimed that "the more wronged, betrayed, or victimized that a man felt, the more likely to have sought custody." (p.300).

A father who has not been the primary parent, but who nonetheless becomes the custodial parent, needs a great deal of help and support in learning to deal with the everyday routine tasks of parenting. Adult men in our society were not raised to focus on their fathering role the way women were raised to mother. They did not have nurturing male role models, were not encouraged to engage in playing at the role of father, and were generally not included in the household tasks of cooking, shopping, and cleaning, or the parenting tasks of carpools, PTA meetings, and arranging for babysitters. A man who did not learn those tasks while married may find himself under a great deal of stress as a custodial father. Then, in spite of his good intentions, he may find himself annoyed with the children and treat them accordingly. Here, as with custodial mothers, a preventive approach is of great benefit to the children. The notion of "first parent, then a divorced parent" is critical.

Men who take on custody also have to learn to communicate with their children on an emotional level. According to Keshet and Rosenthal (1978), the American father's role is frequently as a "doer," who is involved in activities with his children. Custodial fathers have to add the dimension of "being" with their children, which includes responding to emotional needs. Many fathers feel threatened by the new role and see it as a threat to their masculine image.

Men in our culture have been expected to outgrow their childhood affectionateness and craving for affection, while becoming aggressive and competitive. Even clinician's stereotypes of mentally healthy men include: very aggressive and not at all emotional, while mentally healthy women are stereotyped as: not at all aggressive and very emotional (Lewis, 1976). Mental health professionals who work with custodial fathers need to first evaluate whether their own perception of healthy men fits that stereotype. Then they need to help the fathers to be comfortable with their own emotions and affectionate feelings, as well as their own capacities to be empathic and caring.

The role of the father in a child's development has been given less importance by researchers, social scientists, and society in general than the role of the mother. However, recent studies have indicated that the father-child relationship has impact on the child's emotional development (Lamb, 1976). Custodial fathers who are educated to understand the normality of a close father-child bond may feel more comfortable assuming the role of primary parent.

Custodial fathers also need help in coping with any discomfort or embarrassment that they feel regarding their family structure. Because custodial fathers are still a minority group, they may be looked upon quizically by people in the community who make assumptions about how the living arrangement came about. They may feel particularly sensitive and vulnerable to criticism if their wives left them. Their feelings of inadequacy as the primary parent can also contribute to their embarassment.

> When Mr. F.'s son was invited to join a group for children of divorce, Mr. F. called the group leader to explain that his son was different from the other children and might not belong. When the leader asked what made his son different, he replied, "He lives with me—his father!"

> The first therapeutic effect of that particular group was on Mr. F. when he learned that 2 of the other 12 children who had been invited into the group also lived with their fathers. He expressed surprise and relief: "I thought my son would feel funny about our family," he said.

> "I guess *you* felt funny about it," was the leader's reply.

Finally, custodial fathers may find, according to the results of a study reported by Keshet and Rosenthal (1978), that their income is lowered because of the demands of childcare. This is a familiar complaint of working mothers. In the Keshet and Rosenthal sample, 17% of the men did not work full time. Twenty-two percent of full-custody fathers and 21% of joint-custody fathers worked less than full time, compared to only 8% of visiting fathers.

> Mr. G. has shared custody of his 5-year-old daughter. As part of the custody agreement, he and his former wife, both of whom work, are committed to staying in the city in which they presently reside. Mr. G. was offered a job at three times his current salary in a city 1,000 miles away. He refused the job because it would have meant giving up custody. The decision was made after he and his therapist worked through the resentment that he might feel toward the child, and his possible expectations regarding her indebtedness to him.

Because the phenomenon of custodial fathers has been so rare, there has been little research comparing the adjustment of children in mother-absent families with children in intact families (Lamb, 1977). Future research in this area will help therapists who work with single fathers to anticipate some of the problems their youngsters will have.

Joint Custody

As of August 1981, 19 states had joint custody provisions (Bureau of National Affairs, *Family Law Reporter*, August 1981, pp.12–13) in their divorce laws, with other states introducing such legislation. Joint custody, which is alternatively referred to as "co-parenting" (Galper, 1978), "cooperative parenting" (Keshet & Rosenthal, 1978), or "shared custody" (Maricopa County Bar Association, 1980), has distinct advantages for the children. Although it redefines the family structure subsequent to a divorce, it does not deprive the children of their relationship with either parent. Research has shown that the vast majority of children prefer to maintain their relationships with both parents (Hetherington, 1979). Joint custody implies that both parents, just as they did when married, share the responsibility for the children's physical, emotional, and social well-being. In that way, although the parents have divorced each other, neither of them is "divorced" from the children.

Joint custody also provides advantages for parents. In contrast to the award of sole custody, there is no "loser" in a joint custody agreement (Calvin, 1981). Joint custody affords both parents the opportunity for some time away from parenting, in addition to the satisfaction of being an active, involved parent. It gives the children solid evidence of being loved by both parents, as well as confirmation that they are not the cause of the divorce.

Joint custody cannot be effectively ordered by the court. It must be decided upon mutually by the parents. The reason is evident: a joint custody arrangement requires agreement between the parents to separate their parenting role from their husband-wife roles. In order to achieve agreement, parents frequently require the support of mental health professionals. Whatever the circumstances that led to the divorce and in spite of the personal animosity between the parties, they must be able to agree to continue to communicate regarding the upbringing of the children if a co-parenting arrangement is to work. Any problems and decisions involving the children are the concern of both parents and need to be considered by both. The *Domestic Relations Handbook* published by the Maricopa County (Arizona) Superior Court (1980), suggests the following guidelines for shared custody:

At a minimum the factors to be considered by the parents and counselor are:

1. The geographical location of both parents.
2. Arrangements regarding the residential requirements of the children.
3. Arrangements for the children's education.
4. Arrangements for the children's religious training, if any.
5. Determinations regarding the children's health care.
6. Arrangements regarding finances to provide for the children.
7. Arrangements for holidays and vacations.
8. Any other factors affecting the physical and emotional health and well-being of the children.
   If major changes arise, such as moving and remarriage, and present child-care arrangements are no longer feasible, the parents shall agree to renegotiate the terms of the plan with the aid of a Conciliation Court Counselor or private counselor prior to any Court action being commenced (p.13).

The New Jersey Supreme Court, in *Beck vs. Beck* mandated "meticulous fact-finding" to determine whether, in fact, the family concerned meets the clearly specified criteria for joint custody set forth by the court (Peterson, 1981). The criteria are:

(a) Both parents must be "physically and psychologically capable of fulfilling the role of a parent."
(b) Each parent must be willing to accept custody although the opposition of one or both parents to joint custody does not preclude an award of joint custody.
(c) While the parents may be hostile to each other, the parents need only "be able to isolate their personal conflicts from their roles as parents (such) that the children be spared whatever resentments and rancor the parents may harbor." The "potential for cooperation," however, "should not be assessed in the 'emotional heat' of the divorce. While parents may divorce each other, the child should not be divorced from each parent.
(d) The financial positions of the parents must allow for the added expense of two separate homes, (estimated by some economists as requiring up to 25% more available income than does a sole custody/ visitation arrangement).
(e) The proximity of the homes must be examined. (While proximity is necessary if school age children are to frequently alternate homes, especially where the children attend a public school, joint alternating custody arrangements can work where parents live hundreds of miles apart when children are of preschool age or are of school age and the alternation of homes comports with the school calendar.
(f) The employment demands of both parties must be studied to ascertain the availability of each party to the children.
(g) The age and number of the children must be considered.
(h) The preference of the children of "sufficient age and capacity" should

be accorded "due weight." (Fact-finding must, of course, include a determination whether the children were unduly influenced by one parent to state an unrealistically or improperly "implanted" preference.)

Joint custody is a philosophy rather than a formula for post-divorce parenting. Ahrons (1980), in a study of 41 parents involved in joint custody, found that "joint" did not necessarily mean "equal." It neither defines the living arrangements nor the amount of time spent with each parent. Individual couples need to work these out to their own advantage. The presence of a professional is helpful during the time when the structure of the arrangement is being developed and later when differences emerge between the parents' attitudes.

A joint custody arrangement generally assumes geographic proximity between the divorced parents. Proximity facilitates communication between family members and mobility between living quarters.

> Mr. and Mrs. H. decided to separate after 18 years of marriage. They met with a psychologist to work out a custody agreement. They seemed able to separate their parenting and marital roles, and joint custody was recommended. Mrs. H. bought a small house a few blocks away from their previous home. The children, who were in elementary, junior high and high school, changed residences every three months. The shift did not mean a change in neighborhoods, school, or friends for any of them. In addition, when the children were in residence with one parent, they still had fair access to the other parent.

> Mr. H. remarried, but the joint custody continued as it had been.

The arrangement described above allowed the parents to go on with their own lives while continuing to actively parent their children. Dullea (1980) reported that when parents are asked whether or not it is bad for children to have two homes, the universal reply is "It is better to have two parents."

Steinman (1981) studied 32 children from 24 families in which parents had shared child-rearing responsibilities and physical custody. Her findings suggest that the most crucial and beneficial components of joint custody for the children are the cooperative and respectful relationship between the parents. In spite of this, one-third of the children in the study felt overburdened and confused by the demands of living in two homes.

> Bob, age 13, was brought by his mother for individual counseling. His school work had recently begun to slip. He reported

difficulty in concentrating. For two years, Bob's parents had maintained a joint custody arrangement, in which Bob was supposed to move between the two households for two-week periods. The system broke down because Bob's father's work took him out of town at irregular intervals. Consequently, Bob frequently had to return to his mother's home for several days during his period with his father. Bob found the uncertainty distressing. He reported to his therapist that he often awakened at night, unsure of where he was.

Bob wanted very much to change the living arrangement, spending mid-week with his mother and visit his father on weekends. He was afraid of his father's reaction to the suggestion. He perceived his father as an emotionally distant, angry person who would cut him off if he suggested the change.

Bob and his therapist discussed his own well-being, his need to protect his father from his feelings, and his fear of his father's reprisal. Then Bob was able to state his case to his parents. The therapist supported his decision in a conference with the mother, which the father declined to attend. Bob's father did, for a time, respond as the boy had anticipated, but Bob's preparation for the reaction kept it from being devastating. After several months, the father softened.

Sometimes legal joint custody in which both parents are involved in decisions regarding children is not equated with physical joint custody. The parents have agreed that one of them will be the residential parent. The difference between this arrangement and sole custody is more evident to the parents than to the children. It means that the residential parent shares the burden of decision making about the children with the ex-spouse. One of the reported advantages is financial: a father who is consulted about whether his child should have orthodontia or go to camp, is more likely to make his child support payments (Dullea, 1980).

Keshet and Rosenthal (1978) recommended that joint-custodial parents continue to use mediators when conflicts arise between them, just as they did in developing their agreement. Obviously, joint custody is not problem free, any more than parenting is in an intact family. But when a mechanism exists in a divorced family for resolution of conflict, the children are likely to benefit.

The same principle applies when conflicts involving the children continue between custodial and noncustodial parents. It is, of course, harder to put into effect under these circumstances, but not as impossible as one might think.

Don, age 12, reported the following incident to his therapist: "I went to visit my father. He was supposed to take me out to dinner at a nice restaurant, but he wouldn't because I wasn't wearing a suit. He told me to go home and tell my mother to buy me a suit. I did. My mother said that she doesn't think I need a suit and I should tell my father to buy me one."

The tale went on. Obviously, Don was being used as messenger between parents. The therapist called Mr. and Mrs. J., who had been divorced for over four years and asked them to meet with her. Both agreed. In the therapist's office, they argued about the clothing allowance and appropriate ways for Don to dress.

The therapist interpreted their need to continue arguing with each other and that their anger was keeping them connected to each other. Then, the importance of keeping Don out of that anger was discussed. The therapist suggested that Mr. and Mrs. J. deal directly with each other in telephone conversations when Don was not present. They were also advised to first consider whether an issue regarding the child was a real one or an excuse to express anger at the ex-spouse.

Subsequent to that meeting, the therapist helped Don to see the role he was playing. He learned to call his parents to task for involving him in their disputes.

Not all divorced parents are as cooperative as Mr. and Mrs. J. When the parents refuse to be seen together, the therapist and the parent who is willing to come in can discuss and work through the same issues. As long as one parent withdraws from the game, it can no longer be played.

Dividing the Children Between the Parents (Split Custody)

Seth, an 8-year-old in a group for children of divorce, always referred to "our" divorce. The other children in the group spoke of "my parents'" divorce, "their" divorce or just "the" divorce. Seth's choice of pronoun was deliberate. When questioned about it, he explained that his two older siblings lived with his mother and he lived with his father. He felt that he had been divorced from his siblings.

Research indicates that the greater the cumulative stress, the more likely the development of pathology subsequent to divorce (Hodges, Wechsler & Ballantine, 1979). Therefore, dividing the children between parents is not recommended. Divided siblings will, as in Seth's case, experience the loss of siblings as well as a parent. If there is continuing hostility between the parents, siblings who are divided are likely to introject the hostility and direct it toward each other. In contrast, siblings living with one parent can provide a support system for each other, helping each other cope with the common experience.

If economic, geographic, or other factors necessitate dividing siblings between custodial parents, those children need additional attention from the parent with whom they reside. The parents need to be attuned and sympathetic to the loss suffered and the mourning that will need to be done.

Changing Custody

Despite the fact that custody rulings are always subject to modification, the decision to change custody is not one to be made lightly. The court may order a change if there has been a significant change in circumstances that bear directly on the child, such as parental remarriage, or illness of the parent. If custody is changed without serious consideration, both parents are likely to be stripped of their authority and manipulated by the children.

> For over three years, an 8-year-old girl had been living with the uncertainty of who would eventually have custody of her while her parents fought through their lawyers and through the courts. The father won custody.

> Within a year following the custody decision, the child told her mother that since she had been living with her daddy, he had not paid much attention to her. She told the mother she now wanted to live with her. The mother, who had been dissatisfied with the custody decision, allowed herself to be manipulated by her daughter's expressed desire to change custody, reinstituted custody proceedings and submitted to the probationary investigation. In the final steps of the process, the child told the judge she wanted to stay with her daddy and said she had never told her mommy that she wanted to live with her instead. The father was awarded continued custody.

> The child had used the parent's uncertainty regarding custody as

a means of getting a great deal of attention from them. A therapist working with this family could have pointed out the child's plea for attention and healthier ways of giving it to her.

If children are led to believe that they are free to change custody at any time, the parents have rendered themselves impotent. The parents can be controlled by the children's threats to leave whenever they are displeased with their parents exercise of authority. One of the major responsibilities of parenthood is the exercise of reasonable authority and discipline, and the undermining of that authority is detrimental to the children. The child who says "I don't have to listen to you. I'll go live with my other parent" has to be told that that option is not available and that there will be negative consequences for disobedience of the custodial parent's authority. It is important that the noncustodial parent not seduce the child away from the custodial parent with the promise of things being better with him or her or by responding to the child's complaints against the custodial parent by instituting a custody suit.

This is not to say that there are not circumstances under which a change in custody is beneficial.

> Mrs. K. had custody of her two sons, ages 7 and 4. She left the state in which she had lived when married in order to be close to her own parents. She sought therapy regarding her older son's infantile behavior. In the course of conjoint mother-child treatment, it became evident that Mrs. K. was herself so dependent as to be unable to meet the needs of her children. The children frequently expressed the desire to live with their father in their old neighborhood. The father was interviewed. He was willing to take custody of the boys. He had relinquished custody because he believed it would be better for the children not to be involved in a custody battle. Mrs. K. had sought custody because she believed she was supposed to as the mother.

> Custody was changed. Follow-up indicated that both boys thrived in their father's care. Mrs. K. continued in therapy until she remarried. With a new husband who was willing to take care of her, she saw no further need to deal with her own unresolved dependency needs. She did, however, recognize that it would not be wise to have more children.

In this case, the original custody decision had been a poor one and the change rectified the mistake.

In other cases, changes in external circumstances precipitate the desire to change custody. For example, if the custodial parent remarries and there is a clash between step-parent and child, changing custody may be advisable. If the custodial parent is moving out of the child's old neighborhood, and the location was an important criterion for the original decision, a change in custody may be in order. Some fathers who did not realize that they could get custody of their children are going back to the court to ask for a change. Sometimes a custodial parent who has been successful and adequate at parenting a young child has difficulty with an adolescent.

> Carol's parents separated when she was 8 years old. She and her 6-year-old sister remained in their family house with their mother, who enjoyed raising them and was able to be authoritative and warm.

> When Carol entered adolescence, her mother found it difficult to set limits. She complained of being unable to handle Carol, who began acting out mildly, cutting school, staying out late, and doing more drinking than her mother wanted. Mother and daughter fought constantly.

> Finally, Carol asked her father, who was remarried, if she could move in with him. The divorced parents consulted with a therapist who helped them work out the conditions under which custody would be changed: that Carol could not decide to return to her mother and that she had to abide by the rules of her father's house, agreed upon in advance of the move. There was a brief period of continued acting out, that subsided with the father's consistent enforcement of rules.

> At the time, the therapist suggested to the father that he might have to allow his younger daughter the same choice. In her junior year in high school she, too, asked to live with him.

Evaluating for Custody

Mental health professionals are frequently called upon by the courts and by attorneys to make a recommendation regarding which parent is better suited to have custody of the children. There are a number of ways in which such experts can increase their effectiveness and credibility, while keeping the needs of the children in the forefront.

Insist on Seeing Both Parents

The attorney for one parent may ask for an evaluation, ostensibly to determine whether the client is a suitable parent. However, since the custody dispute is an adversary procedure, the real question is whether the client is a more suitable parent than the other parent. Clearly, no one can make a comparative judgment having seen only one parent and relying on that individual's view of his or her adversary. Many professionals allow themselves to be placed in that position by seeing only one parent. If the case goes to court, the professional is likely to be embarrassed on the witness stand by the attorney for the individual who was not seen. A negative answer to the query, "Did you see my client?" invalidates the expert's testimony.

When the request for custody evaluation comes from an attorney, the evaluator has an opportunity to serve as an advocate for the children. Attorneys are bound to take their client's position. That does not preclude their recommending that the client change his position. Therefore, the professional who accepts the role of custody evaluator can wonder what the attorney will do if it is not recommended that his client be the custodial parent. The evaluator can elicit a promise from the attorney to try to change the client's position, in order to do what seems best for the children. Not all attorneys are willing to relinquish the adversarial position, but an increasing number of attorneys are.

In seeing both parents, the evaluator has the opportunity to explore the sincerity of each one's desire for custody, the feelings engendered by possible loss of custody, their capacity for parenting, and so on. During the interviews, each parent can be prepared for the possibility of loss of custody. In most cases, both parents are reasonably fit and both need to understand that loss of custody does not imply that he or she is unfit but rather that the other parent presented some advantages to the children (Warner & Elliot, 1979). Nevertheless, the psychological impact of losing custody can be powerful, and may lead to depression or a loss of the sense of self (Schuman, 1981).

It is helpful to see each parent with the children. Part of the custody evaluation will be interviews with the children. If each parent has the opportunity to bring the children in, the evaluator is able to observe the interaction between parents and children.

> Mrs. M. was seeking custody of his 9-year-old son. His attorney sent him to a psychologist for an evaluation. The psychologist saw both parents alone and then asked each of them to bring the child for a session. The child reacted very differently with each parent. With the mother, the child was rigid, talked little, seldom made eye contact and sat on the far side of the couch. With his

father, the child smiled, seemed relaxed, and spoke about plans he had made with his dad. The psychologist asked the mother to bring the child a second time to help determine the consistency of the child's behavior in his mother's presence, ruling out unusual situational circumstances. The child's behavior proved consistent. The child's apparent comfort with his father and discomfort with his mother led the psychologist to further question aspects of the mother-child relationship. Although denied by the mother, reports from other agencies and father and son reports indicated the possibility of previous maternal abuse and neglect. The psychologist recommended that the father receive custody.

Interviewing the Children

The evaluator's task in interviewing the children is to ascertain their preference and determine with which parent the children have a healthier relationship, without giving the children the impression that the custody decision will be based solely on their statements. The evaluator can surmise the preference for custody indirectly, by exploring the ways in which time is spent with each parent; what is liked and disliked most about each parent; which parent is generally sought when there is a problem, and so forth. Psychological testing can provide evidence of children's relationships with both parents. Also, as previously noted, direct observation of the parent-child relationship in the evaluator's office provides invaluable data.

Keeping Therapist and Custody-Evaluator Roles Separate

The professional who is the therapist to one of the litigants is clearly not an unbiased evaluator and should refer the custody evaluation to someone else. When the parent or parents of a child client request a custody evaluation, it is recommended that the therapist refer them to a colleague in order to keep the therapist and evaluator roles separated. The reason for not serving as a custody consultant when a child is in treatment is that the therapy is likely to be jeopardized (Gardner, 1976). The parent who loses custody is bound to be angry at the therapist for the recommendation and may sabotage the child's therapy by expressing the hostility overtly or covertly.

Conversely, the professional who has served as an evaluator in a custody case, is advised not to accept any of the parties for treatment, in order to maintain a position of neutrality. Custody cases may be reopened at any time and the therapist who is treating any of the parties is no longer an impartial evaluator.

Conclusion

The determination of custody is a decision crucial to the children of divorcing parents. It is a decision which needs careful thought and guidance to separate the feelings between the parents from the needs of the children. Mental health professionals can help parents explore their motives and understand the ramifications of various custodial arrangements. They can mediate in ongoing disputes over custody. They can, most importantly, focus the parents' attention on what is best for the children, from whom they are not being divorced.

Chapter 6

Helping Parents
Deal with Visitation

But will you still take me to McDonalds?
—Judy, age 7

A concomitant of the award of custody to one parent is the establishment of a means by which the noncustodial parent can have access to the children. The means is referred to as visitation. The terms of visitation are generally included as part of the custody decision, whether made in or out of court. The noncustodial parent is usually assigned "reasonable visitation rights," although these are not clearly defined. In a study of 63 families, only 1 in 7 respondents reported input from legal sources as important to visitation agreements, and only 2 in 63 reported input from a counselor as important (Alexander, 1980). The proposed Uniform Marriage and Divorce Act includes the following provisions regarding visitation:

> (a) a parent not granted custody of the children is entitled to reasonable visitation rights unless the court finds, after a hearing, that visitation would endanger the child's physical health or significantly impair his emotional development.
> (b) the court may modify an order granting or denying visitation rights whenever modification would serve the best interests of the child; but the court shall not restrict a parent's visitation rights unless it finds that the visitation would endanger the child's physical health or significantly impair his emotional development.

Expert Opinion on Visitation

Goldstein et al. (1973) strongly opposed the concept of free visitation. They proposed that the custodial parent should have the right to decide whether or not the noncustodial parent should visit the child. Their goal was the protection of the relationship between the custodial parent and the child.

Subsequent experts have disagreed with the Goldstein, Freud and Solnit position. Gardner (1976) considered the recommendation dangerous, potentially placing "lethal weapons in the hands of children or incompetents" (p.355). He foresaw enraged parents unilaterally cutting children off from the noncustodial parent.

Wallerstein and Kelly (1980) found that children of divorce passionately and persistently yearned to have contact with the absent parents. However, in the majority of instances, "reasonable visitation rights" were interpreted to mean twice-monthly weekend visits, that the children in their study found woefully inadequate. The intense longing for greater contact persisted for many years after the divorce. Rosen (1979), in a study of 96 children, found that 69% would have chosen free access to the noncustodial parent. She concluded that children's sense of well-being is undoubtedly affected by restricted access.

Jacobson (1978c) studied the effect of time lost in the presence of the father on 51 children, ages 3 to 13, from 30 families. The fathers had spent an average of 53.6 hours in the presence of their children in a two-week period prior to the separation, compared with an average of 20.12 hours after the separation. Jacobson found that the more time lost with the father, the greater the maladjustment of the child in the areas of aggression, inhibition, cognitive disability, and overall severity of maladjustment, as measured by the Louisville Behavioral Check List.

Although access to the noncustodial parent is healthy for children, it is not as widely available as might be expected. In a study of 560 divorced parents, Fulton (1979) found that only one custodial parent; in five reported a steady pattern of visitation by the noncustodial parent; 44% reported a tapering off of visitation, 6% reported once or twice a year visiting, and 28% reported that there was no visitation at all. Almost 40% of the custodial mothers admitted to actively preventing access to the children for reasons that were punitive in nature.

In Support of Frequent Visitation

Recent research leads us to take a position in favor of frequent visitation by the noncustodial parent. The inability of a person to function well as spouse in a family does not, in our view, preclude the individual's adequate functioning as a parent in that family.

There are, of course, exceptions that have to be carefully considered. Henszey (1976) reviewed court instances of denial of visitation. Failure to pay support clearly does not justify denial of visitation. The child's apparent indifference to visitation is judicially considered but does not control the court decision. When acts, threats, or fear of physical violence are extreme, visitation rights will generally be denied, although there have been cases where courts have refused to deny visitation in the presence of child abuse. Only the "most base form of sexual or moral conduct" (p.219) will threaten visitation rights. In the case of abandonment or lapse of time between visits, courts vary in their decisions.

> When Mrs. A. learned that her former husband was beating their children (ages 11 and 8) with a paddle during visits, she went to court and asked that visitation be suspended. The judge did suspend visitation and required that the mother, children, father, and father's girlfriend become involved in counseling. The judge recognized that he had no jurisdiction over the father's girlfriend, but suggested voluntary cooperation in the interest of all parties.

There are times when the noncustodial parent's presence appears detrimental to the child, and is not.

> Mr. B., divorced by his wife, harbored tremendous hostility toward her. He particularly resented her freedom to date other men. One day he angrily entered her apartment, scissors in hand, and cut off her hair unevenly, telling her that no man would find her attractive anymore.

> Mrs. B. went to her lawyer to get a court order to keep Mr. B. from visiting their 10-year-old daughter. Mr. B. submitted to a psychiatric evaluation, that determined that he was not a threat to the child. His aggressive behavior toward his wife was viewed as "controlled" by the psychiatrist, and visitation was therefore continued.

Visitation must be perceived as *for* the chidren rather than as *against* the custodial parent. The children are not divorced from the noncustodial parent. A parent living outside the home is still the child's parent.

The problem for many divorced parents is that visitation means contact between them, over the phone to discuss visiting plans, and in person at the time of the visit. The anger and hostility that led to the separation and may well have been exacerbated by the divorce process frequently still exists between them. The contact regarding visitation is probably second only to contact regarding money as a vehicle for expressing the continuing anger. Frequently, the two are interdependent, with the withholding of money as a weapon in one parent's hands and the withholding of visitation privileges the other parent's weapon.

Mr. and Mrs. C. had been separated from the time that their daughter was 6 months old. Mr. C. was very erratic in sending his child support payments. Whenever the check was late, Mrs. C. would refuse to let him visit the child. Mrs. C. brought her daughter for therapy when she was 8 years old, because the child was bed-wetting. It became obvious that she wet her bed whenever she had expected a visit from her father and had been deprived of it by her mother.

The therapist requested that Mr. and Mrs. C. come in together, which they did. The child-support issue was successfully separated from the visitation issue. The therapist helped Mrs. C. to recognize that her refusal to let her ex-husband see the child had not produced the desired result, which was to have Mr. C. send the check on time. Mr. C. was helped to recognize that his withholding of the check was a way of continuing to express anger at his ex-wife. When they had acknowledged the motives for their behavior, Mr. and Mrs. C. were able to agree that Mr. C. would be allowed to see his daughter at regular intervals in spite of late payments. Visitations became predictable and the child's bed-wetting ceased.

As long as visitation is the undeclared battleground, the children are likely to lose out on contact with the noncustodial parent. A major task of a therapist working with any members of a divorced family is to separate the husband-wife relationship from the father-mother relationship, in order to increase the likelihood of frequent, regular visitation.

Divorced parents often deny that they have any feelings of connectedness with the former spouse. They are surprised at the interpretation that although they no longer love each other, their anger toward each other serves to keep them connected. Before they can relinquish the anger, it may be necessary to work through the need to remain attached. In addition, the use of visitation as a way to express the hostility is frequently unconscious and needs to be brought into conscious awareness in the therapeutic sessions. Then it becomes possible for the parents to express hostility directly toward each other.

Mr. and Mrs. D. had been divorced for several years. Mrs. D. had remarried and Mr. D. was living with a woman. They both believed that because they had started new lives they had no interest in or feelings about the former spouse. However, hardly a week went by that didn't produce arguments between them over visitation, frequently pulling the children into the middle.

The children were becoming more and more distressed, rarely knowing whether father would show up or mother would allow a visit.

On two occasions, the parents came in together to see the older child's therapist. The therapist wondered if there was anything either parent was angry about but had failed to express. Mrs. D. was furious about the fact that her husband had left the family for another woman. She had expressed her anger at his leaving the family, but had never spoken of her personal hurt and fury at having been "tossed aside for another woman."

The two sessions allowed Mr. and Mrs. D. to ventilate some old angers. At the same time, they learned to deal directly with each other without involving their children.

Flexibility: The Key to Harmonious Visitation

The structure of visits has a great influence on what happens during them. Therefore, it is important to look first at how visits are set up.

Visitation agreements often specify the frequency, the day, and the length of the visit between noncustodial parents and children. That kind of rigidity is bound to lead to displeasure on the part of all those concerned. Most adults and children find it difficult, if not impossible, to be inflexibly tied to a schedule that allows for no other plans to arise. Unfortunatley, the greater the hostility and distrust between parents the more likely that a rigid, detailed visitation schedule will be established (Gardner, 1976).

Accommodating the Child's Schedule As Well As the Parent's

When visitation is on a fixed schedule, the child's needs are forced into conflict with the parent's needs. For example, Sunday is a frequent fixed visitation day for noncustodial fathers. What happens when a child is invited to a birthday party on Sunday? Some visiting parents are hurt and angry if their children choose another activity over a visit. If they express their feelings, the children are faced with a conflict: either choose the party and feel anxiety or choose the parent and feel deprived.

Parents need to be helped to understand that it is healthy for children to pursue their own activities, even after their parents are separated. It may help to point out to them that if the family were intact, they would expect and welcome their children's development of independent outside activities.

In order to accommodate parents and children, it is helpful to have the scheduling of visits stated in a way that implies flexibility. Some examples are:

1. Noncustodial parent will take the children on Sundays unless that conflicts with anyone's other plans, in which case another convenient day will be arranged.
2. Noncustodial parent may take the children one evening a week, and one day over the weekend, at everyone's convenience.
3. Noncustodial parent will take the children at least 6 times per month, with agreeable times to be decided upon at the beginning of each month.

There is an increase in flexibility from 1 through 3. The kind of statement will depend on the postseparation relationship between the parents. The therapist's task is to move them toward acceptance and tolerance of the more flexible visitation plan.

In addition to allowing for leeway in day of visit, the therapist should encourage flexibility in length of visits. Besides making it possible to accommodate other plans, arranging visits of varying lengths is helpful in preventing visits from becoming monotonous and tedious for parent and child.

Understanding the Changing Needs of a Growing Child

As children become older, part of their normal development includes spending more and more time with peers. Parents of adolescents often comment that their children are only at home to eat and sleep. Although there is some exaggeration in that statement, it does point to the changing need for parental contact as children get older.

It is sometimes hard for divorced noncustodial parents to appreciate that the reason their children are not interested in seeing them as much as they did is their normal developmental thrust rather than a personal rejection. Therapists can help them to see that older children also spend less time with the parent with whom they live. Recollections of how they themselves spent time away from their families as they matured also make the point.

The style and schedule of visitations has to change to meet the needs of older children. A teenager is more likely to agree to dinner on a week night than to spending Sunday afternoon at Dad's house. By recognizing the changing needs, the parent is less likely to experience rejection or the hostility of a youngster who has felt compelled to acquiesce to parental demand.

Seeing the Children Separately

Some visitation agreements force the visiting parent to take all of the children on every visit. There are a number of reasons why such rigidity is undesirable. All of these reasons reflect the importance of recognizing the individuality of the children.

First, the everyone-visits-together model does not allow for any of the children to have something else to do on the day of the visit.

Second, it does not permit the visiting parent to plan activities geared to the individual needs of the child. We can assume that children of different ages within a family would prefer different activities, and that siblings will have different interests, talents, and dislikes that need to be recognized.

Third, the everyone-visits-together model makes it very difficult for the parent to give individual attention to one child. Within a household, there are natural opportunities for one child to be alone with a parent. It may be bedtime, or getting help with homework, or going shopping for new clothes. Children need and enjoy the attention of parents without siblings around. The visiting parent and the child should not be deprived of that facet of the parent-child relationship.

Finally, the solo visit is likely to be very pleasant for the parent because there is no opportunity for the children to fight with each other.

> Mel, age 11 and his 8-year-old brother, Ed, always visited their father and his new wife together. Mel complained to his therapist that his stepmother did not like him and was much more attentive to his younger brother.

> On one occasion, Mel's father was called away on business, leaving his wife with a pair of tickets to a play. She invited Mel. He wanted to go to the play, but was reluctant to go with his stepmother. He decided to risk it and much to his surprise, had a thoroughly delightful time. He developed a new basis of a relationship with his stepmother. It did not hold up to his satisfaction when Ed was around, but it was considerably improved. He then observed that his stepmother really didn't avoid him; the truth was that Ed was more assertive in getting attention for himself.

Mel began to learn to ask for what he wanted, a skill that Ed already had. Mel then requested that some visits be arranged for him without his brother.

Other Considerations

Visits Should be Predictable

Children whose parents have divorced have gone through a period of uncertainty and change. Subsequent to the divorce, it is important to re-establish stability in children's lives. The establishment of a predictable, dependable pattern of visitation is part of the rebuilding process. It may be undermined by either parent. Or, as Wallerstein and Kelly (1980) noted, the children's behavior may contribute to the erratic visitation, especially the typically angry behavior of 5- to 12-year-olds. Predictable and dependable does not have to mean rigid. It does mean that when a date and time for a visit have been set, it is adhered to. It does mean that there is a regular pattern to the frequency of visits. The goal is to establish a balance between the need for predictability and the need for flexibility in visits.

Visits Should Not be Used for Spying

Divorced couples frequently maintain a curiosity about each other's activities. The visitation process provides an opportunity to find out, via the children, what the ex-spouse is doing. It is particularly uncomfortable for children to be quizzed about the other parent's social life.

Jack complained to his peers in a divorce group that whenever he returned from a visit with his father, his mother gave him the third degree. She asked: "What is his girlfriend like? Is she pretty? Is she intelligent?" and so forth. Jack did not want to answer the questions but he didn't know how to tell that to his mother without arousing her anger, with which he was very uncomfortable.

Role playing a discussion between he and his mother, in which he told her that he would rather not be asked questions about his father's life style, helped Jack to anticipate his mother's responses and his reaction. He was able to go home and tell his mother what he was feeling and reported to the gooup that his mother was reasonably cooperative subsequent to the discussion.

One of the reasons that it is helpful for a parent to be in concurrent treatment is that when an issue such as this comes up in the child's therapy, the therapist has the opportunity to explore the parent's perceptions and motivations and help the parent to change the behavior. When the children are part of a group, the group leader may have to arrange a parent conference if the child is not as successful as Jack was in achieving the goal.

Sometimes, the child enjoys the spy role because it meets with great parental approval. In such instances, the role will only be relinquished when the parents are made aware of its detriment to the children and stop reinforcing it.

Parents Using Visititation Time to Ventilate Anger at Each Other

The pick-up and drop-off times of the visit provides an opportunity for face-to-face contact between parents. It gives them a chance to continue the battle and play out the anger, jealousy, and feelings of rejection associated with the divorce. Wallerstein and Kelly (1980) reported that one third of the children in their sample were exposed to intense parental hostility at visiting time.

For the children, the anticipation of their parents' hostile behavior puts a damper on the whole visit. They are as uncomfortable when their parents fight at visits as they were preseparation. They may try to get away from the scene or to act as mediators, depending on the role they had in the earlier phase.

If the parents cannot meet without expressing anger, a neutral pick-up and drop-off arrangement may have to be developed. The simplest is to have the children ready to leave as soon as the doorbell rings or car horn sounds. All arrangements must have been attended to prior to the visit.

The therapist working with divorced parents needs to focus on the unresolved anger so that the visitation period does not remain a battleground indefinitely.

Helping the Visiting Parent

Although they have the title of "mother" or "father," the job description of visiting parents is changed by virtue of not being present in the household to deal with the day-by-day issues of child rearing. The role becomes more like grandparent than parent. Grandparents extol the advantages of their status. They claim to have all the pleasures from the children, without the aggravation. They admit that they are not as close to their grandchildren as they were to their children. It is the potential lack of closeness that makes the visiting parent's role unenviable. On the surface, it appears easy and more desirable than being the custodial parent with the bulk of the responsibility. But the trade-off is high in losing the strong, intimate relationship with the children.

Being a "Real" Parent

The parent who has left the children is often beset by guilt (Gardner, 1976; Wallerstein & Kelly, 1980). In order to assuage the guilt and reduce the likelihood of rejection by the children, the parent frequently assumes a Santa Claus role, bestowing gifts upon the children and acceding to most of their demands. This role has deleterious effects on all of those involved. The visiting parent feels used and financially taken. The custodial parent feels angry at being unable to compete with the "good," giving visitor. The children are spoiled and their frustration tolerance is reduced; although if asked, most children would express approval of the generous visiting parent.

"Real" parents are *not* agreeable and giving all of the time. They say "no," get angry at their children, need to do some things for themselves, and leave children to entertain themselves. "Real" parents are not expected to be "on" all the time.

The therapist can help the parent out of the Santa Claus role. The first step is therapeutic, working through guilt feelings that underlie the behavior. As long as those feelings exist, the parent is unlikely to be able to respond to the therapist's suggestions to treat the children differently. The second step is educational, teaching the parent to behave and respond as a "real" parent.

Because their time with the children is limited, visiting parents may overdo their involvement with them. They may keep the children at their side throughout the visit. They may play with them or take them places every minute that they are together, creating an uncomfortable and unnatural parent-child relationship.

> Mrs. E. was allowed to visit her 6-year-old son every other Sunday for 4 hours. During that time period, the child often wanted to play with his neighborhood friends. Intellectually, Mrs. E. understood the child's need to create an atmosphere similar to that which he had known when he lived with her. However, in therapy she discussed her difficulty allowing the child to be away from her during "her time." She wanted his exclusive attention during visits to alleviate some of her feelings of loss.

The visiting parent who is helped to approximate family living in the visit is more likely to be satisfied with the visiting arrangement and to establish realistic relationships with the children.

Mr. F. had been divorced for 6 years. He visited with his children weekly. The children spent one weekend each month at his house. Mr. F. found the weekend easy and comfortable. Being at home with the children felt natural and they all went about their business, coming together irregularly and spontaneously.

Mr. F. complained to his therapist about the quality of the other visits. The children lived too far away to bring them to his house for an afternoon. "How many movies can we see or games can we bowl or hamburgers can we eat?" he asked his therapist.

One of the solutions that the therapist helped Mr. F. to find was to make the visiting schedule more flexible. Mr. F. began visiting on days when his son had a ballgame that he could watch or his daughter had a gymnastics exhibition. The children perceived him as more involved in their lives and he felt less pressure to create activities for them.

Spending time in the visiting parent's home rather than going places provides a fertile atmosphere for the development of a real parent-child relationship. Within the home, there are activities such as the preparation of meals, watching a TV show, or fixing a household item, that provide comfortable opportunities for interaction. Being in the parent's home also allows time for parent and child to be away from each other. Although a visit may seem too short to consider being separated during it, there is less pressure on all those involved if they do not have to spend every minute together. The natural flow of coming together and separating, as in an intact family, establishes a basis of a real relationship. Among other ways to establish a real relationship that the therapist might suggest is to have the child:

1. Bring homework along on the visit.
2. Bring a friend along some of the time.
3. Be a part of the planning for the visit.
4. Invite the visiting parent to share his or her school or extracurricular activities.

At the other extreme are visiting parents who consider it enough to be in the child's presence during a visit. They take the children to work with them and let them play or just watch. They take the children along to social functions and leave them to their own devices while they socialize. They bring along their dates and focus their attention on them, rather than on the children.

Mr. G. picked up his 8-year-old daughter faithfully every other Sunday at 9 A.M. He took her directly to his parent's home and left her there, while he pursued his own activities. At 5 P.M., he collected her and returned her to her mother. Although he fulfilled his obligation to take his daughter, he was rarely a parent to her. The child told her therapist that she didn't care if Daddy came or not.

The therapist conferred with Mr. G., shared the child's feelings about his visits, and explored his motives. Mr. G. wanted to be a good father, but did not know how to achieve this goal. He was referred for help to an adult school parenting program and to Parents Without Partners.

Visiting parents of this sort are more likely to be fathers in traditional fathering roles who never developed intimate relationships with their children. Their lack of direct involvement with the children makes them dependent on the family unit for their sense of fatherhood (Keshet & Rosenthal, 1978). These parents need to learn the basic parenting skills that they did not acquire when the family was together.

Being an Involved Parent

Visiting parents easily become outsiders in the children's lives. Because they are not in the home, they do not receive school notices or hear the daily reports of planned activities for Scouts, Little League, dancing school, or Sunday School.

Jill, age 11, complained to her therapist that her father never came to any of her school plays. It seemed that she would tell him about the play a day or two before the performance and he inevitably had business plans that he could not change. Jill was angry and disappointed.

The therapist suggested to Jill that she tell her father of an upcoming event as soon as she learned of the date, giving her father sufficient notice. Jill was doubtful that her father would come, even under those circumstances. She was surprised and delighted when her father came to her next show, given three weeks notice.

In this case, the child had the responsibility for involving her father in her activities. Many children will not take the initiative and instead suffer the feelings of being rejected by a disinterested parent. To avoid that situation, visiting parents need to be encouraged to assume the responsibility and to invite the children to keep them apprised of their activities.

Many visiting parents of school-aged children are not aware of their rights in relation to schools. In this regard, it is important to know parents' rights under the Family Educational Rights and Privacy Act of 1974 (FERPA). The statute provides that school districts must provide parents access to records that educational agencies and institutions maintain that are directly related to the students. (Postsecondary schools must provide such access to students themselves). Under the law, who is a parent? The Department of Health and Human Services (formerly HEW) interpretation was:

> One can best understand the FERPA position on parents rights if he separates the concept of custody from the rights that the FERPA accords parents. Custody or other residential arrangements for a child do not, in themselves, affect the rights of the child's parents under the FERPA. The FERPA deals with a parent's rights of access to and control over a child's education record.
>
> For the purpose of the FERPA, a school district must accord a natural parent the rights the Act accords him or her unless the courts or a responsible party has provided it a legally binding document that specifically removes that parent's right to have knowledge about and participate in his or her child's educational process. (Custody and parent rights under the FERPA, HEW).

A liberal interpretation of the rights of noncustodial parents to school records allows them the right to see copies of report cards and be informed about school functions via school notices and bulletins. Unless the court has specifically denied that right to noncustodial parents, they should be encouraged to exercise it. In that way, they will be more involved with their children and remain "real" parents. Knowing how their children are doing in school and what is happening there helps the visiting parents to be a part of a major aspect of their children's lives.

Planning the Visit

Visiting parents can make the task of planning the visit considerably easier if they involve the children in it. Discussions of what activities would be mutually enjoyable give indications to the parent of how to spend the time together meaningfully. The child who has contributed to the planning is more likely to be enthusiastic about the activity and to feel motivated to participate in it.

The parent who lives outside of the home may easily lose sight of the child's interests and growth. Plans made unilaterally may then prove unsatisfactory to the children and dampen their interest in being with the parent.

> Mr. H. brought his son to therapy. The boy was a 13-year-old who engaged in minor antisocial activities. In attempting to improve the father-son relationship and to keep his son closer to home, the father purchased a car to rebuild but then complained that his son had quickly lost interest. It was found that the rebuilding project met more of the father's needs than the son's. The type of car was one the father liked and had chosen to work on and the father only allowed his son to watch rather than take an active participatory role. The son continued to find more interest in antisocial activities with his peer group. Through the therapeutic process, Mr. H. gained awareness of how his self-centered perception of his son's needs alienated the boy and how, by only allowing the boy to watch, he conveyed the message that the boy was incapable of helping, which angered him. The insights led to a change in the father's behavior. He and his son began to engage in mutually satisfying activities.

When the Children Do Not Want to See a Parent

We have already noted several examples of situations in which children do not wish to see their parents. Visiting parents can generally tolerate a few cancellations for other plans, and, as mentioned, can learn to tolerate their growing children's reduction in interest in them.

Sometimes children adamantly refuse to see a parent. The pain for that parent is tremendous.

> Mr. I's wife left him after 20 years of marriage, taking their two adolescent children with her. Mrs. I. and the children refused to have any contact with him. Mr. I. was embarrassed, perplexed, and hurt by his children's behavior. He believed that his wife had in some way brainwashed the children against him. He felt helpless to do anything because his children ignored any attempts he made to contact them by phone or letter.

> Mr. I., in therapy, reviewed and explored his own behavior toward the children and was able to reduce the guilt that had been causing much of the pain.

In this case, it appeared that the mother had indeed strongly influenced the children against their father.

Sometimes, in exploring the visiting parent-child relationship, the visiting parent becomes aware that his or her own behavior has created the rift. A child in an intact family cannot escape from a punitive or authoritarian or disinterested parent, but a child of divorce can sever the relationship with a visiting parent who behaves in that manner. When a parent becomes aware of the behavior and feels willing and able to change it, he or she then is faced with the task of communicating the realization to the child and convincing the child that things will be different in the future.

> Sixteen-year-old Loretta was the youngest of three daughters. Her older sisters were out of the house and she was in her father's custody. Loretta perceived her mother as cold and narcissistic, unable to give to her children. She had returned to law school when Loretta was 4, and pursued a high powered career as an attorney.

> After the separation, Loretta refused to see her mother at all, using the refusal as a way of "getting even." Her mother was so distraught at losing husband and child, that she agreed to enter therapy in an effort to change herself. Six months later, she approached Loretta, acknowledged her own shortcomings, and beseeched her to visit. Loretta at first refused, enjoying the power she felt over her mother, but several weeks later, she agreed to meet her for dinner.

Frequently there is a lack of communication between visiting parents and their children, so that neither parent nor child knows if the others are dissatisfied. Opening lines of communication is a necessary step to understanding and preventing breakdowns in the visitation process. If communication is well established, the parent is better able to assess the source of the child's disinterest in visiting. In order to resolve the problem, the parent has to define it. The problem may be the visiting parent's behavior, or the child's changing needs, or the influence of the custodial parent. When the problem is the custodial parent, the child is merely a pawn. The problem cannot be solved by visiting parent and child, but needs to be contended with by the divorced couple.

The End of a Visit

Every visit ends with a separation between parent and child. For some children, the separation continues to create uncomfortable feelings for a long time. Many parents respond with a "you shouldn't be sad" approach, because they are uncomfortable with the child's expression of feelings. The parent who tells a child not to feel sad or not to cry denies the feelings and makes the child feel wrong for having them. A better approach is to acknowledge the child's discomfort, allow its expression, and perhaps even join it, saying "I feel sad, too, when we have to say goodbye. But I feel better when I think about seeing you again soon."

Helping the Custodial Parent Deal with Visitation

The custodial parent has a number of problems to contend with in regard to visitation, including: relinquishing control of the children to the ex-spouse, making contact with the ex-spouse, dealing with the children's feelings and behavior before and after visits, and reacting to differences in values and ideas regarding child rearing. The extent to which all of these loom as problematic is very much related to the amount of hostility existing between the parents. Single parents who are able to feel friendly toward their former partners are fortunate (Weiss, 1979). The further along the continuum from hatred toward friendliness that ex-spouses are, the less intense the problems and conflicts over visitation will be. The therapist working with a custodial parent will do well to focus first on reducing the hostility and then dealing with any specific issues of visitation that have not been resolved in the process.

Manipulating the Child's Desire to Visit

Custodial parents may, consciously or unconsciously, manipulate the children's desire to see their other parent and/or the availability of the other parent. Sugar (1970) noted how the phrasing of a question can put doubt in a child's mind: "You don't *really* want to go visit with your father again on Sunday?"

> Mrs. J., who had custody of her two sons, ages 8 and 4, thought of her ex-husband as uneducated and inferior to her. She vehemently denied conveying her attitudes toward her children and expressed surprise that the older boy was reluctant to visit his father because there was nothing to do. Exploration with her therapist revealed that whenever the boy came home from a visit, she asked him to describe his activities. She would respond with the observation that the day must have been dull or boring. When confronted by her therapist with the message she was transmitting, Mrs. J. replied, "But it *must* have been boring!" The therapist queried, "To whom?"

Some custodial parents make other plans and fail to have the children available for the visit. They are likely to attribute their action to forgetting, but the unconscious motivation for the memory lapse needs to be explored. Concrete reminders, such as keeping a "visiting calendar," in a place where the children can also see it, can help prevent repetition of the behavior while the unconscious problem still exists.

A few parents deliberately keep the children and their other parent apart, in spite of divorce or separation agreements that permit visitation. These parents are allowing their own feelings to interfere with the relationship between the ex-spouse and the children. Custodial parents sometimes move their children to geographically distant locations to accomplish their own goals.

> Mr. and Mrs. K. had separated after he informed her of an affair he had been having. After the divorce, Mr. K. married the woman with whom he had had the affair. Mrs. K., unable to emotionally recover from the loss of her husband, frequently disallowed visitations or "forgot," in the fear of also losing her son who felt close to his father.

Here, as in many of the situations that we have discussed, the therapist's task was to separate the parent's feelings from the needs of the children.

Disruption of Home Life

A custodial parent may manipulate the visitations because of the perceived impact on life at home. The child who has just returned from a visit with a Santa Claus-type parent may expect the same from the custodial parent. The child may be harder to control after such a visit and may taunt the parent at home with the expression of the wish to live with the other "nicer" parent. It is difficult for custodial parents to be cast in the role of the "mean" parent. They may be tempted to be as nice as the former spouse, to the detriment of the child.

> Joel's 4th grade teacher complained to the school psychologist that Joel would not obey any classroom rules and got very little work done. A conference with his mother revealed that she had made no demands on him at home since his father left some 6 months earlier. She explained that his father was very indulgent and she didn't want Joel to love him more than he loved her. The school psychologist explained the importance of limit setting and its impact on a child's love was discussed. Joel's mother began to set limits at home and his classroom behavior improved markedly.

Some parents become excessively strict in an effort to counteract the indulgent parent. It is difficult for custodial parents to maintain their own values regarding child-rearing in response to an indulgent visiting parent. Custodial parents can be helped to assume an attitude of, "That's okay when you're with your other parent, but here at home you know what I expect of you and what you can expect of me."

The custodial parent may resent having to deal with the child's feelings subsequent to a visit. Children may come in angry, sad, frustrated, elated, enervated, exhausted, and so forth. Sometimes the feelings persist for several days. If the custodial parent blames the ex-spouse for having caused the child's feelings, rather than perceiving the feelings as originating in the child in response to a situation, then he or she is likely to be particularly unsympathetic to the child. By shifting the focus from the cause to the child's reaction, the therapist will help the custodial parent to remain empathic and supportive to the child.

Handling the Child's Disappointment

It is the custodial parent's task to help the child whose other parent has failed to appear for a scheduled visit. The custodial parent is likely to be as angry and disappointed as the child, but there are different approaches to dealing with the feelings. Some parents convey their own annoyance and in that way validate the child's feelings. If it is limited to the specific situation and not generalized to everything about the other parent, it is healthy and helpful. Some parents are afraid to say anything negative about the former spouse, even when it is called for. They deny their feelings and the child's, leaving the child confused and guilt ridden for having been angry or disappointed.

When a visiting parent has a pattern of not appearing, it is helpful for the custodial parent to play down the impending visit and discuss the possibility that it may not materialize. The children are not set up for disappointment.

> Nine-year-old Michael waited at the door for his father to visit. He was freshly bathed and dressed and excited about his evening out with Daddy. He sat at the window, staring at every car that passed. His mother went about her chores, ignoring what was happening with Michael. Finally, after over an hour, Michael went to his room and went to sleep.

> For several days afterward, according to his mother, Michael was sullen and sluggish. The therapist noted that he seemed depressed and wondered why the mother hadn't talked about what had happened. "I didn't want to remind him," she replied. The

therapist pointed out that the mother was joining in the child's denial and helped her to understand why her behavior was detrimental to the child.

Conclusion

Visitation is a long-lasting issue among the parties to a divorce, ensuing from the time of the separation to the children's achievement of maturity. It is frequently the arena in which old hostilities between spouses are played out. The therapist who works with divorced parents singly or together, must focus on dissipating the hostility and separating the problems of visitation from it.

Children who have continued frequent access to their noncustodial parents are happier and better adjusted than children who are deprived of their parents. The therapist's goal is to move the parent and children toward the most frequent interaction possible, unless the individual parent's presence is harmful to the child.

Chapter 7

The Impact on Children of Parental Dating and Remarriage

Can the daughter of my father's new wife be my sister?
(Whiteside & Auerbach, 1978)

The Thrust toward Remarriage

Four-fifths of the people involved in the breakup of a first marriage through divorce are expected to remarry. For those whose first marriage ends in divorce, the median length of time between divorce and remarriage is about three years (Spanier & Glick, 1980). Forty percent of second marriages, as opposed to 33% of first marriages, end in divorce. The nation's step population now includes 6.5 million stepchildren under age eighteen.

Spanier and Glick (1980) reported on the results of a demographic study of remarriage. They determined that white women are more likely than black women to remarry. "White women most likely to remarry are those whose first marriage was relatively brief, who were under 30 at the time of the divorce, who were married at a relatively young age, who had no children or only a small number of children in their first marriage, and who had less than a college education" (p.296). The greater the number of children she had, the less likely a woman was to remarry. Women with three or more children are less likely to divorce and one reason may be that they are aware of their lessened prospects for remarriage.

After divorce, the individual enters a kind of second adolescence, complete with changes in roles and self-percepts. Also contributing to the analogy to adolescence is the resumption of dating. After having settled down to a one-to-one relationship, the divorced person is once again exploring and experimenting with new partners. The divorced parent has the additional task of integrating the new or regressive developmental stage with the ongoing responsibility of parenthood. For many parents and children, dating and subsequent remarriage bring another set of problems to an already traumatized family.

Parental Need for Socialization

Hetherington, et al. (1977) studied 96 divorced families with young children. Their subjects complained that socializing is organized around couples so that recreational opportunities are limited for single adults. In this sample, although social life increased for divorced women in the two years subsequent to divorce, it always remained lower than for married women.

Divorced men and women experience intense feelings of loneliness (Hetherington et al., 1977). The loneliness includes feelings of inner insufficiency and feelings of anxiety or tension (Weiss, 1979). Restless activity, loss of sleep, and longing for the ex-spouse may accompany the loneliness. Sometimes, when loneliness becomes chronic, there is a movement toward depression. The obvious cure for loneliness is the establishment of a new relationship.

Divorced men and women also report varying degress of sexual tension (Weiss, 1979) experienced apart from the loneliness. Men whom Weiss studied seemed likely to accept the correlation between sexual deprivation and sexual tension, whereas women tended to separate themselves from their physical needs. In the Hetherington et al. (1977) sample, men seemed to show a peak of sexual activity in the first year after divorce. In the past few years, with the influence of the women's movement, we are finding more and more divorced women who perceive their sexuality in the way previously attributed to men.

In the initial period following divorce, men and women are likely to seek relationships that will offer support and be unthreatening (Taibbi, 1979). Old friends and extended family are more likely to be sought than new relationships. New relationships are distrusted and intimacy is likely to be avoided during this transitional period.

> Mrs. A., after a year in therapy, was able to move out of her house, leaving behind a verbally and physically abusive husband. She took an apartment within walking distance of her previous house to give her children, who stayed with the father, access to her. In therapy, she fantasized about resuming a relationship with a man she had known before her marriage. In reality, she was unable to embark on any heterosexual relationship because of her residual anger toward and distrust of her husband, which she generalized to other men. It took several months of working through those feelings before Mrs. A. felt ready for a date.

In the next phase, the individual is likely to begin to experiment, to get a new perspective on his or her own image, sexuality, and interpersonal style. By the end of a year, divorced men and women expressed the desire for greater intimacy and a dissatisfaction with casual sex (Hetherington et al., 1977).

The Effects of
Parental Dating and Remarriage
on Children

Like the effects of the divorce itself, there are a number of variables that influence the effect of dating and remarriage on the children. First is the age and developmental level of the children. A second critical factor is the degree to which the divorce trauma has been resolved by the child. Another important issue is the relationship between parent and children and the degree to which that relationship appears threatened by the dates and/or remarriage. Finally, the custodial parent's problem with dating is more complicated than the noncustodial parent's because of the presence of the children and the need to consider their reactions.

Age of the Children

At each age, there are developmental tasks to be accomplished. Parental dating and remarriage superimpose additional stress on the developmental tasks of childhood, and in that way, serve as potential crisis events (Thies, 1977).

The preschool children in the Wallerstein and Kelly (1980) study frequently responded to their parent's divorce with a general neediness, expressed in a random reaching for new adults. For such young children, a new parent figure offers a model for identification, badly needed to further development (Tessman, 1978a). In the home of the custodial parent, an emotionally needy young child is likely to cling physically to the dates who come and implore them to become a new parent. Custodial parents may respond with embarrassment or anger, while their dates feel pressured and leery.

The 6 to 8-year-olds whom Wallerstein and Kelly (1980) studied yearned acutely for the absent parent. Boys who lived with their mothers urged them to remarry so they would have fathers. A date coming into a home with a 6 to 8-year-old is frequently pressured to become a new parent.

In contrast, 9 to 12-year-olds (Wallerstein & Kelly, 1980) were notable for their anger. Their anger might be expressed when dates appeared, either at the parent or the date, making it uncomfortable for the adults and sometimes succeeding in discouraging the parent from dating. Children at this age show fierce loyalty to the absent parent and are creative in developing strategies to fend off intruding potential step-parents (Tessman, 1978a).

For latency age children (ages 6–12), parental dating and heightened sexual activity disturbs the normal development phase of quiescent sexuality. Some latency age girls are thrust into a precocious adolescence and many children begin to seek older companions over their peer group. Many latency age children are preoccupied with sexual thoughts and fantasies (Wallerstein & Kelly, 1980).

> David, age ten, was referred for individual therapy because he was having difficulty falling asleep and could not concentrate on his homework. His mother's remarriage coincided with onset of symptoms.

> David acknowledged that his sleep and homework were disturbed by his listening for noises from his mother's bedroom, next door to his. At first he denied knowing what the noises were. Then he admitted to their sexual content. Finally, he dealt with his own sexual feelings toward his mother that had been intensified during the three years in which he saw himself as "man of the house."

> When the sexual conflict was resolved, sleep and homework no longer presented a problem. Some time later, David's mother became pregnant. David, aware of how he had learned to cope with his sexual feelings, remarked to his therapist, "Can you imagine how upset I would have been if this had happened *before* I came to you?"

Adolescents have a particularly difficult time coping with parental dating. The developmental tasks of adolescence involve emerging sexuality and developing identity. Preoccupation with sex and marriage is normal. However, it is greatly intensified when the parents cannot be perceived as old and sexless, but are rather behaving in a manner similar to the children.

Parents may have difficulty setting limits on their children's sexual behavior when they themselves are involved in nonmarital sex (Sorosky, 1977). Adolescents experience feelings of competition with their parents or their parents' dates. If they perceive their parents as choosing someone else over them, they may too easily equate the choice with sexual activity and become sexually active themselves (Tessman, 1978b). Later, they discover that the sexual activity did not provide sustaining love.

Following their parent's remarriage, it is common for teenagers to experience sexual feelings toward stepsiblings and step-parents. The feelings need to be acknowledged and accepted, but not acted out (Visher & Visher, 1979). Girls in homes with stepfathers are particularly at risk for sexual acting out. Kalter (1977) suggested that this family constellation is potentially explosive because of the lack of the incest barrier between stepfather and daughter. Some adolescents respond with timidity and fear when living with an unfamiliar adult or stepsiblings who bring up uncomfortable feelings related to previous experience. Unpleasant affect associated with someone else may be projected onto the step-parent.

> Karen, a 14-year-old was brought to individual therapy by her mother, who expressed concern about her daughter's moodiness. From the time the mother had announced her impending remarriage three months earlier, Karen had been slamming doors and refusing to talk. There was no immediate provocation for her behavior. She reportedly liked her mother's fiancé and got along well with his son.

> In therapy, Karen was able to discuss the time when a man exposed himself to her and to connect that recollection to her fear of living in an intimate atmosphere with an unfamiliar man and his 16-year-old son. Her moodiness was an expression of the fear which she had not acknowledged to herself. When she did, she was able to discuss the feelings first with her therapist and then with her mother. When the marriage took place, Karen accepted it without a recurrence of the moody behavior.

At the time of remarriage, many adolescents feel usurped by the new same-sex parent. The new man in the house may take on responsibilities that were previously the province of a teen-aged boy. In addition, the adolescent is faced with the conflicting tasks of becoming an integral part of a new family unit and loosening emotional ties with the family (Visher & Visher, 1979). For example, adolescents in intact families balk at going on weekend trips with the family. They prefer to make their own plans with peers. An adolescent in a reconstituted family wants to establish a place within the new constellation. To refuse to go with the family on a weekend trip is to risk not having a place. To go on the trip means giving up the opportunity to be with peers and move toward autonomy.

Resolution of Divorce Trauma

Thies (1977) hypothesized that the resolution of divorce trauma, particularly grief, is a major determinant of the way in which a child will adjust to the parent's remarriage. The child who has had the opportunity to express feelings, particularly grief, at the time of the parents' separation is more likely to be able to cope with parental dating and remarriage and their implications.

Although dating and remarriage appear to replace a lost love object for the child, they also serve as a reminder of the loss. The date or step-parent is *not* the absent parent. Indeed, the presence of a new parent may serve to drive the noncustodial parent further away. Dating, and particularly remarriage, validate the finality of the divorce. A child who has been sustained in the postdivorce period by reconciliation fantasies, will have to abandon the fantasies in the face of reality. If mother has a new husband, she cannot marry father. The child is forced to deal with that reality and may experience an exacerbation of grief and even a regression to immediate postdivorce symptoms.

When one parent remarries, the children must also cope with the other parent's responses. Just as children's unresolved feelings are intensified by the remarriage, so are those of ex-spouses. Hetherington et al. (1977) found that remarriage of the spouse was accompanied by reactivation of feelings of depression, helplessness, anger, and anxiety. At such times, as in the immediate postseparation period, it is important for mental health professionals to focus the parent on the parenting role.

Mrs. B. brought her 8-year-old daughter, Sarah, to therapy. The child had read *The Boys and Girls Book about Divorce,* after which she informed her mother that she had some things she wanted to discuss with a psychologist. The mother responded by contacting a therapist and arranging an appointment for her daughter.

Sarah drew a picture of her family, but became confused about including her father's wife-to-be in her drawing. The child asked whether the therapist was going to show the picture to her mother. Her concern was related to her mother's feelings about the father's forthcoming remarriage.

Mrs. B. was being seen concurrently in individual therapy. She began to understand the effect her negative feelings about her ex-husband's marriage were having on her daughter and she recognized that her relationship with her daughter was being jeopardized. She worked through the feelings of rejection and hostility that were connected to her husband's remarriage. She stopped expressing the hostility to her child. She was able, several months later, to dress her daughter in preparation for the father's remarriage. The child reported that she came back from her father's wedding and told her mother all about it. She no longer had to protect her mother from the information or herself from her mother's reaction.

Post-divorce Relationship between Parent and Child

Researchers (Visher & Visher, 1979) have noted that the bond between custodial parent and child frequently becomes more intense than that between parent and child in an intact home. In part, this is a natural concurrent of not having a second adult with whom to share the responsibilities of parenthood. Both the parent and the child may contribute to the greater intensity in the relationship. The child who has lost one parent, is likely to hold onto the parent who remains. Gardner (1970) made the comparison to a one-eyed man who worries about something happening to his good eye, leaving him blind. Some children develop symptoms of school phobia as a result of their need to be monitoring the custodial parent's presence at all times.

The custodial parent may unconsciously use the child in place of the absent spouse, as someone on whom to rely. Thus, a male child may be given his father's responsibilities for heavy chores, and be perceived as the "man of the house." When the parent is tense, only the child is there for comfort. At times, children and parents reverse roles and the children are given the responsibility for making their parents feel better. A custodial mother who does not socialize may unconsciously use her son as the object of sexual fantasies (Sugar, 1970).

When such a strong bond has developed, regardless of what the impetus to it has been, dates are likely to be perceived as intruders who want to displace the child in the parent's affection. The child is likely to respond with overt hostility, making it difficult for the adult relationship to continue.

> Mr. C. invited his girlfriend to live with him and his 18-year-old daughter. The daughter made the couple's life miserable. She incited arguments, became sloppy around the house, disregarded all requests made of her by the girlfriend, and was generally obnoxious. The girlfriend sought a therapist's advice. She was at the point of giving up her relationship with Mr. C. because she could not tolerate what was happening. Mr. C. decided to tell his daughter to leave instead. The girlfriend, although relieved, felt very guilty. The daughter's worst fear, that her father would replace her in his affections, was confirmed.

To prevent the development of this kind of situation, the custodial parent must be made conscious of the parent-child relationship and keep it appropriate. Particularly with opposite sex parent and child, the Oedipal implications of the relationship need to be explored. The parent needs to be helped to maintain authority and independence so as not to stimulate the child's fantasies.

If the parent seeks help after the relationship has over-intensified and is interfering with dating or remarriage, the therapist's task is to help the parent return to a normal parent-child relationship. At that point, the child may need to be involved in therapy as well.

Dealing with Issues Around Dating

Helping Parents Prepare Children
for Parental Dating

The more communication there is between parents and children regarding the idea of dating, the less likely there is to be unpleasantness among the parties involved. The communication must be two-way, with the parents explaining why they want to socialize with their peers, and the children encouraged to reveal their anxieties, distrusts, and hopes.

> Mrs. D. reported to her therapist that she frequently planned activities with her date that could include her daughters. At the last minute, her 14-year-old would refuse to go and mother and daughter would fight. The therapist wondered if mother and daughter had ever discussed the girl's feelings. Mrs. D. came to her next session greatly relieved. Her daughter had acknowledged that she just didn't wish to be involved with mother's boyfriend unless the relationship came to marriage. Mrs. D. realized that she had been trying to recreate a family for her child to absolve her own guilt, rather than in response to her daughter's needs. She stopped planning those kinds of activities and instead found time to do things alone with her daughter.

The parental explanation must vary with the age of the child and must be appropriate to the child's level of understanding. You may recall the story of the 6-year-old who asked his mother where he came from. The mother launched into a complete explanation of human sexuality. The baffled child responded, "No, Mommy—Charlie comes from Texas. Where do I come from?"

Young children can understand their own desire to play with their peers and can use that to see their parents' needs. They can recall their own family when there were two parents or may see parents of friends operating as couples. They can be told that men and women have special good times together. They may need assurance that their parents will continue to love them, even if the parent begins to love another adult. Older children may need help to understand that dating relationships are private, and that just as they have private thoughts and times, so must their parents (Gardner, 1970).

Mental health professionals can help parents with their responses to the children's communications regarding dating. Some parents avoid the communication totally so as not to have to contend with their children's hostile feelings about their dates. Some go even further, and sacrifice their social lives so as not to experience the children's anger. These parents need help to tolerate the anger. Other parents, guilty over having exposed their children to the divorce, are fearful of making their children unhappy again. If the children express the slightest unhappiness about the dates, the parents respond by not going out. They need to realize that their avoidance behavior is placing their children in control of them and undermining their authority. When a child displays anger or unhappiness about parental dating, the parent needs to recognize and acknowledge the child's feelings, explore their origin, and help the child overcome them. In that way, the parent is neither ignoring the child's feelings nor being controlled by them. At the other extreme are parents who, in response to their children's apparent hunger for a new parent, rush into a marriage to meet the professed need. Gardner (1976) warned that marrying for the sake of the children is ill-advised as staying together for that reason. The new marriage is unlikely to be successful if it is based on the children's needs and the effects of a poor second marriage would be more traumatic to them than living with a single parent.

Deciding Whom the Children Should Meet

Parents re-entering the singles' world are likely to date a number of individuals before establishing an ongoing relationship. They may see some dates only once or twice. For the children, exposure to a series of such people is confusing and frustrating. They cannot understand the reason for the succession of partners and cannot be expected to relate well to them. For the boy with a divorced mother or the girl with a divorced father, the string of rivals exacerbates the feelings of competition.

> Mrs. E. was separated from her husband for about six months when she began dating. Her daughters, ages eleven and nine, wanted to meet all of Mommy's boyfriends. Her 14-year-old son would tell her to have a good time, but would manage to be upstairs doing his homework or listening to the stereo when mother's date arrived. Mrs. E. was sensitive to her son's feelings and made no attempt to force him to interact with the dates.

"When there's someone I'm really interested in, that will be time enough," she said.

The situation is somewhat different for the custodial and the non-custodial parent. The latter can more easily keep casual, transient dates from the children.

Custodial parents. When a relationship does become less casual and one individual is being seen frequently, then the children should be involved. Otherwise, the parent is splitting life into two distinct segments. The children are likely to perceive the split as putting them on the outside. They are sure to be aware of the parent's involvement and distraction from them. If they are totally excluded, they are likely to be resentful of the individual who is taking the parent's attention. Should a marriage ensue, the relationship between step-parent and children would be off to a poor start.

Visiting parents. Children covet the time they spend with a visiting parent. It is finite, frequently perceived as too brief, and consequently, very precious. It is therefore difficult for children to tolerate a date along on the visit.

> Jack, age twelve, was unhappy that his father always brought a girlfriend along on visits. "He asks *her* what she wants to do or where we should have dinner. He never asks me," he complained to his therapist. Rather than be continually subjected to feeling like an unimportant person, Jack began to resist going out with his father. Jack's therapist called the father and suggested that he spend some time alone with his son. The father had been unaware of his son's displeasure. He admitted that he had a better time with a date along. For him the date served to cover his inability to relate to his child.

When the noncustodial parent becomes involved in a long-term relationship, then it is appropriate to include the children in it. However, some time alone with the children is still advisable.

Helping the Parent Whose Child
Makes a Scene
When a Date Arrives

Some children will fuss or scream when the parent leaves with a date. The mental health professional can first ascertain from the parent whether the child has been adequately prepared for the parent's dating. It is unlikely, if the groundwork has been laid, that such behavior will occur. But some children are more determined than others!

If such behavior does happen once, before the next date, the parent should re-examine the subject with the child. Then the parent should firmly establish that regardless of the child's behavior, he or she is going out. It is important that the parent be consistent and do what he or she had said. The parent who backs down will be disbelieved in the future. The parent who stays home in response to the child's behavior has reinforced the tantrums, saying in effect, "The reward for your tantrum is that I will stay home."

The Date Who Stays Overnight

We have discussed the overtness of sexuality in new relationships that children of divorced parents are more likely to experience than are children with long-married parents. The awareness is heightened when dates stay overnight in the parent's bedroom, when the parent stays out all night with a date, and when the parent vacations with a lover. It is advisable to limit these experiences to partners with whom a long-term relationship has been established. Obviously, the children should no more be exposed to observing or hearing sexual activity than they should with their married parents.

In the home of the custodial parent.   In this area, the custodial parent bears greater responsibility to the children because they are living in the same home. Many custodial parents make it a rule not to have their lovers stay in the house as a protection for their children's feelings. Weiss (1979) found many custodial mothers who adhered to this policy in order to maintain their own credibility in teaching values about sex to their children. He also found that men are less concerned about the obviousness of their sexuality to their children than are women (Weiss, 1979).

When a date is going to stay over, children should be told beforehand, so they are not surprised at finding the individual in the house in the morning. Here, as in telling children about so many subjects, it is important for the information given to be sufficient without going beyond the bounds of discretion. For most children, it is enough to say that a special boy or girl friend will be staying over because he or she and the parent like each other very much and they want to spend as much time together as possible. The same kind of explanation can accompany the statement that a parent is staying out overnight or vacationing with a date.

Adolescent children as previously noted, have the greatest difficulty coping with their parent's overt sexuality.

> Mrs. F.'s boyfriend slept over several times a week. Her 16-year-old daughter, Ann, was very aware that every time he stayed, he and her mother were sexually active. To her therapist, Ann

denied being uncomfortable with the sexuality, but said that she just couldn't stand the guy because he was an ex-Marine and bossed her around.

Ann became sexually promiscuous at this time, even to the point of prostitution. The therapist met with Mrs. F. with Ann's permission, but the mother refused to acknowledge any connection between her behavior and her daughter's.

Ann ran away. She knew no other way to escape from the overly stimulating home environment.

In the home of the noncustodial parent.   The sexual activity of the parent who does not live with the children is less obvious to them. Unless it is flaunted, it need not be an issue at all.

Mrs. G. refused to let her 13-year-old son stay overnight at his father's apartment. She told the boy the reasons: "Your father's girlfriend lives with him and sleeps in his bed. I don't want you exposed to that."

The son found the reasoning ridiculous. "I already *know* she sleeps there," he told his therapist. "My father told me. So what's the difference if I stay? I won't stay in Dad's room!"

Parents who are aware of the impact of their heightened sexuality are less likely to be overstimulating or seductive toward their children. In that case, the children can be expected to be better able to cope with and integrate the parental sexuality.

Living Together

In recent years, different life styles have gained increasing acceptance in our society. For many people, living together without being married is a comfortable alternative to marriage. For some, it is perceived as a preamble to marriage or a testing ground. For others, it is the only relationship intended, allowing a degree of psychological independence not associated with marriage. Divorced individuals who have already experienced an unsuccessful marriage may be hesitant to enter another. For them, living with someone seems less threatening.

Parents need to consider the impact on their children of their choice to live with someone, rather than marry. It is important for parents to consider the community in which they live, its attitudes toward cohabitation, and the feedback which the children are likely to experience. If there is likely to be teasing or scorn from neighborhood peers, as there may be in some conservative communities, parents would do well to prepare their children for it.

Perhaps the most difficult task is to establish the role of the unmarried partner toward the children. Can he or she tell the children what to do, discipline them, or give permission? Once the partners have decided, the children must be told clearly. Even with step-parents, children frequently refuse to acknowledge the authority and the tendency is more pronounced with a live-in partner. When the child says, "I don't have to listen to you. You are not my father/ mother," that adult needs a basis of authority from the child's parent.

Dating and the Homosexual Parent

In recent years, as homosexuality has become more accepted and public, increasing numbers of people divorce in order to pursue a homosexual relationship. The heterosexual parent is often loathe to expose the children to the homosexual parent.

Gardner (1976) noted that children's sexual identity is fairly well established by age 3 or 4, and that homosexual parents did not seem to produce homosexual sons at a higher rate than did heterosexual parents. Therefore, keeping youngsters from their homosexual parents seemed unnecessarily cruel. However, the homosexual parent needs to be at least as diligent as the heterosexual parent in keeping sexuality private. This is especially true for pubescent children.

> Mrs. H.'s former husband, a homosexual, had the right to take their son for the summer and had done so for several years with no problem. When the boy was twelve, the father proposed spending the summer with him in a resort community known for its homosexual clientele. Mrs. H. went to court to get an order forbidding Mr. H. from taking the boy that summer, unless the plans were changed. After conferring with a psychologist, the judge so ordered, citing the boy's age as the reason.

When a homosexual custodial parent chooses to live with a partner, many of the problems are the same as those experienced with a heterosexual live-in relationship. However, the homosexual pair has the additional problem of allowing the children to develop their own sexuality and not drawing them into homosexuality. Some lesbian couples share a house, but keep separate bedrooms in order not to flaunt their sexuality in front of the children. One lesbian mother continued to maintain separate bedrooms even after her son had married. She explained that she was thinking ahead to grandchildren. Interestingly, although she purported to be satisfied with her own homosexuality, she did not want it for her progeny. This is consistent with Gardner's (1977) contention that most of the homosexuals he encountered would prefer that their children be heterosexual.

Gardner (1977) recommended the following guidelines regarding visitation and custody rights for a homosexual parent: "The greater the degree to which the child is exposed to a homosexual environment, the greater should be the restrictions imposed to protect the child from the detrimental effects of such exposure" (p.268). The child should be spared the confusion and anxiety that exposure to homosexuality is likely to engender.

Dealing with the Immediate Problems of Remarriage

It is not within the scope of this book to cover all the issues and problems associated with parental remarriage and reconstituted families. The interested reader is referred to *Stepfamilies: A Guide to Working with Stepparents and Stepchildren* by Emily B. and John S. Visher for a more extensive look at the subject. We shall consider the preparation of children for the parent's remarriage, handling their reactions to it, and anticipating some of the problems which will ensue.

Preparing the Children for the Remarriage

Children are probably no less aware of a parent's impending remarriage than they were of the impending divorce. They pick up cues around them even when they are not told what is happening. Just as it was important to clarify the issues around the divorce, separating fantasy and reality, it is important for parents to discuss the remarriage with the children.

Parents should be encouraged to inform the children and to be prepared to listen to and respond to the children's reactions. Parents who expect a completely joyful reaction are likely to be disappointed. Although they themselves are experiencing positive, hopeful feelings upon entering a new marriage, they must be prepared to tolerate ambivalence and even decidedly negative feelings from their children. If they are helped to understand the reason for the children's feelings, they will be better able to cope with them.

If children are decidedly negative toward the parent's intended new spouse, the parent should explore the possibility of the validity of the feelings. With a therapist, the parent can explore such questions as:

• Am I insensitive to something about the person I'm marrying that the children recognize?

- Am I getting married to allay loneliness or provide my children with another parent, rather than because of what I feel toward this person?
- Am I marrying someone just like my former spouse?

The parent who is clear about feelings toward the new spouse and motivation for marriage will be better able to deal with the children's responses. To consider and deal with negative reactions from the children does not mean to give up the new marriage. Here, as in dating, the parent cannot relinquish so much control to the children.

In preparing the children for the new family structure, other changes in lifestyle must be acknowledged. To begin with, remarriage requires that the family that has reorganized subsequent to the divorce must again struggle with the process of reorganization (Messinger & Walker, 1981). The parents need to consider that each additional change acts as a potential stressor. If the new marriage will mean moving or changing schools or the addition of the new spouse's children to the home, the children need to be aware and to be given the opportunity to respond.

> Ed, age nine, lived with his father and an older brother. When his mother left the home, Ed saw her frequently. He adjusted well to the new situation. His home, his friends, his school and even his housekeeper had not changed.

> Suddenly, Ed began reporting that he was unable to sleep. His anxiety stemmed from his awareness of his father's growing involvement with a woman who lived some 30 miles away. Nothing had been said about a remarriage, but the prospect of moving away from his environment and from his mother created more distress for the boy than had the parental separation.

> When Ed's mother became aware of her son's anxiety, she confronted her former husband and asked him to be more open with the children about his plans.

Children's Concerns about Remarriage

End of the reconciliation fantasy. When a parent announces the intention to marry someone new, children are faced with the finality of their parents' divorce. Obviously, if one parent has a new partner, there is no way for mother and father to get back together. Some children have defended against the pain of divorce by holding onto the reconciliation fantasy. Its demise removes the defense and leaves them exposed to the pain.

With such children, parents can anticipate a return of the immediate postseparation behavior. At times, the children may even appear to have more problems than when the separation occurred. It may be difficult for them to give up a wish that has sustained them for a period of time.

Oedipal rivalry.   For some children, having a single opposite sex parent has allowed the flourishing of a great deal of Oedipal fantasy material. If the parent has moved the child into a position of the "man" or "woman" of the house, as previously discussed, the fantasies have been encouraged.

When the parent announces the intention to marry, the intended spouse is perceived by the child as a victorious competitor for the parent's love. The child feels vanquished and is likely to be very angry at the parent and new spouse. The child is likely to experience strong feelings of inadequacy.

> Twelve-year-old Bob hated his new stepfather. He attributed his feelings to the man's personality, especially his bossiness, and his "ruling the roost." Bob's mother insisted that those were inaccurate perceptions of her new husband.

> After a period of therapy, Bob began to discuss material that was clearly Oedipal in nature. He recalled having had surgery to enlarge his ureter at the age of three and related the memory to concerns that his penis was too small.

> With the awareness of those feelings of competitiveness with his stepfather for his mother's attention and working them through in therapy, Bob changed his view of his stepfather and was able to relax and enjoy the new family.

I don't like him/her.   Some parents expect that because they are in love, their children will love or at least really like, the new individual. That is an unrealistic expectation for a number of reasons. Children who have experienced parental loss through divorce are frequently hesitant to invest their feelings in a new person, for fear of re-experiencing the pain. Children look for different qualities in adults than do their parents, so that a step-parent may not be instantly likeable. Step-parents may themselves demand too much instant liking from the children, causing further withdrawal (Visher & Visher, 1979). Finally, the child may well be conveying "You are not my real parent and I want my *real* parent." When a child says "I don't like him/her," the parent may need help in understanding just what the message is. Understanding the communication will help make the response appropriate.

The parent who can be tolerant of the child's feelings and not insist on his or her liking the step-parent is off to a good beginning. The parent who can convey an attitude of, "I know it takes time and you don't like your step-parent yet" is giving the child room to develop positive feelings. The parent who verbalizes that this new spouse does not have to displace the absent parent in the child's affection is recognizing the child's concern and need to hold back.

Will it happen again?   Children today, even when their parents have not divorced, do not experience the same sense of security within the family as children did just a generation ago. When only celebrities got divorced, children could tolerate their parents fights or disinterest in each other without concern that a divorce was imminent. Today's children frequently ask their parents, "Are you getting a divorce?"

For the child who has already experienced a divorce, the security of family life does not exist. The fear that a new marriage will end as did the first one is understandable. However, many parents are reluctant to deal with the children's concerns because they arouse their own anxieties along the same lines. Avoiding the subject does not alleviate the anxiety for anyone. Therapists can help parents to face their own fears and then to communicate with the children.

Anticipating Post-remarriage Problems

Parents who understand the problems that commonly ensue after remarriage can take a preventive approach and lessen the likelihood of such problems emerging. If problems do emerge that require therapeutic intervention, it is recommended that the step-parent be an integral part of the treatment.

Divided Loyalty

Wallerstein and Kelly (1980) observed that "where the child experienced painful psychological conflict that he or she was unable to resolve between the love for the father and the love and loyalty to the stepfather, the adults were likely to be pulling hard in opposite directions" (p.294). When the parent and step-parent were not in a competitive position, the children in their sample seemed able to integrate all of the adults into their lives.

Mr. I. indicated to his therapist that his 3-year-old son was distressed by the presence of Mommy's new husband, Joe. He said that the boy spoke of Joe all the time, and that meant that he was unhappy. He was planning to tell his ex-wife to keep Joe away from the child.

The therapist wondered whether Mr. I. wasn't feeling displaced in his wife and child's affections by Joe. Mr. I. acknowledged that he was and that it made him angry. He realized that he was trying to influence the child to dislike his stepfather.

There are some remarried couples who expect the children to renounce the noncustodial parent as a condition for acceptance into the newly structured family (Wallerstein & Kelly, 1980). The children are placed in a conflict situation. Parents who make such demands need help in keeping their hostility toward the ex-spouse from their children and allowing the children their own feelings.

When a noncustodial parent is inattentive and unloving, the children are drawn to the step-parent. However, they may fear that their attachment to the step-parent will drive their own parent further from them. Parents can help in this situation by absolving the children of the responsibility for the absent parent's behavior.

Establishing the Role of the Step-parent

When a family is reconstituted, one of its tasks is to establish the roles of its members within the household. It is fairly simple to determine who now does certain chores, like taking out the trash or clearing the table. A more difficult task is the establishment of new lines of authority. Children who have been accustomed to answering to a single parent frequently resent the new spouse's attempts to set rules or to demand adherence to them. It is not unusual to hear, "You are not my father. You can't tell me what to do."

Some remarried parents attempt to resolve the problem by maintaining the task of discipline themselves. As far as the children are concerned the new spouse is then an impotent member of the household. Other remarried parents readily abdicate their authority to the new spouse and some new spouses attempt to take over the disciplining entirely. In these instances, the new spouse is likely to be perceived by the children as intrusive and out of place and adherence to the rules is unlikely.

Most successful are those newlyweds who have discussed their notions of childrearing, have agreed on what is expected of the children, and are prepared to be consistent in their approach to the children. This is not an easy task, because the partners may have very diverse views about childrearing. In addition, it is impossible to anticipate all the decisions that will have to be reached. Consequently, ongoing communication between the new partners about childrearing is essential. The children need to be told that the step-parent is fundamentally in agreement with the parent and has been designated authority by the parent. In this way, the reconstituted family can offer the children the consistency between parents which is essential to good parenting.

What's in a name?   Children sometimes have difficulty in deciding how to address a step-parent. They feel disloyal if they use the name reserved for the absent parent. A parent might suggest an alternate form of address, such as "Pop" if the natural father is called "Daddy." The issue should not be forced by the parents who need to understand what the word represents to a child. Many children find it more comfortable to call a step-parent by his or her first name. Step-parents frequently report that after they have been in the household for a period of time, the children modify the form of address as an acknowledgement of affection that has developed.

When children reside with a remarried mother, they are confronted with having a different surname from the mother. They have to explain to teachers and friends that their mother's name is different. The mothers need to be sensitive to any discomfort that this creates for the children and help them develop ways of responding to questions or teasing. Some remarried custodial mothers change the children's name on school records, although that is illegal. The children's name stays that of the father unless they are adopted by the stepfather. Adoption by the stepfather is not recommended unless the natural father has disavowed or disowned his children.

Extended Families

When a parent remarries, children acquire a new set of relatives; grandparents, aunts, uncles, and cousins. The integration of all of the people into the children's lives cannot be expected to happen instantaneously. The new relatives may need to be reminded to approach the children slowly.

On the other hand, the relatives of the noncustodial parent feel that they lose the children. Grandparents are especially sensitive to the emotional and sometimes physical distancing of their grandchildren. It remains the responsibility of the divorced mother and father to allow the lines of communication to remain open between the children and their grandparents.

Conclusion

Like the effects of divorce, there is no uniform reaction to parental dating and remarriage. There are an enormous number of variables determining the children's reactions.

Parents who are alert and sensitive to their children's needs and responses can reduce the likelihood of distress for their children during the period of their dating and if and when they remarry. Parents who are willing to focus on the children's needs even during their own time of neediness and self-involvement are, by their willingness to do so, reducing the likelihood of negative reactions. As at the time of the divorce itself, the key is, "Don't forget the children."

Chapter 8

The Influence of Values on Professionals, Parents, and Children

Actions are governed by values; values are beliefs regarding what is right and wrong for oneself and for others. In this chapter, we shall look at the influence on the client of the mental health professional's values regarding divorce, the influence of parental values on their children, and the impact on children of changes in values brought about by divorce. Mental health professionals, as are all people, are influenced in their decisions and actions by their values. In spite of trying to respond according to what is best therapeutically for the client, it is not possible to be uninfluenced in responses by one's values. Therapists query clients according to what they believe it is important to know. Comments are made in response to the client and interpretations are made. The therapist communicates nonverbally with a frown, a smile, a hand gesture, a posture. Even a neutral facial expression or absence of a hand shake communicate something. It is therefore important to be aware of one's own attitudes and how they might influence the client-therapist relationship.

The mental health professional needs to explore his or her own values about divorce. Values communicate information about the professional to the clients and may foster certain value changes in the clients. More specifically, the mental health professional can explore his or her attitudes regarding marriage as a sacrosanct agreement, circumstances under which marital separation and divorce are acceptable, the role of the child, behavior of separated parents, parenting, communication, causes of divorce, and the question whether or not divorce is good or bad in general, and what is best for whom.

During the formative years, all children are exposed to and assimilate the value systems of their parents and others important to them. Values are also transmitted via the culture, numerous personal experiences, and input from the mass media. With whom and with what children identify is based on innumerable factors as are their degree of value flexibility and their need to communicate their values to others.

Value conflict is experienced when a real-life situation challenges or threatens what was taught (incorporated values). For example, a divorcing client may create conflict within the mental health professional who believes that marriages should never be dissolved under any circumstances.

Mental health professionals who have experienced their own divorces have first hand experience with the upheaval in values that a divorce creates. Certainly, as with other problems confronted, first-hand experience is not necessary in order to understand, empathize, and help. However, professionals experiencing divorce, or who have unresolved issues about their own divorces or the status of their marriages, need to be especially aware of countertransferential issues. The following two examples demonstrate the interference of unresolved issues on the part of the helping professional.

> Dr. A., a well-trained and sensitive therapist went through a divorce. Her husband had been repeatedly unfaithful. Soon after the separation, the therapist evaluated a male patient who had engaged in extramarital affairs. Dr. A. referred the patient to a different therapist because she was aware of her own anger toward the patient; she knew she needed to deal with her own feelings before she could effectively work with such a patient and be able to separate her issues from the patient's.

> Mr. B., an attorney, saw a couple together for a relatively simple no-fault separation and divorce. The couple had compromised on a settlement and wanted the attorney to expedite the legalities. The attorney felt himself in sympathy with the husband, that he was being taken advantage of by the wife, and began to encourage the couple to revise their settlement with more property given to the husband. The settlement process began to become conflictual until the lawyer realized that the woman reminded him of his own estranged spouse; then he was able to separate his own situation from what was best for this couple and return the proceedings to a nonconflictual level.

In order to explore one's own values regarding divorce, the reader can respond to each of the following statements as True (T) or False (F):

1. _____ People who are unhappily married should stay together for the sake of the children.
2. _____ Mothers should have custody of their very young children.

3. _____ Fathers cannot emotionally nurture children as well as mothers.

4. _____ Mothers will spend more time with their children than will fathers.

5. _____ Joint custody is preferable to either the mother or father having sole custody.

6. _____ Fathers remarry sooner, causing an additional adjustment for the children.

7. _____ Divorce always has a negative effect on children.

8. _____ A child should live with the parent of his or her choice.

9. _____ Parents should not provide reading material about divorce unless the child requests it.

10. _____ The custodial parent should control extent of visitation.

Regardless of whether the given answers were "True" or "False," a firm response indicates a bias of which the reader can be aware. When the reader finds a strong bias, several options are available. First, the basis of one's values can be analyzed to determine the degree of flexibility for change and the needs these values are based on. Second, the clients can be referred elsewhere (as Dr. A. chose to do), if it is determined that the values will interfere with therapeutic effectiveness. Third, the professional can still work with the client, but might state his or her values at the outset, allowing the client the choice of working in this situation.

The Impact of the Therapist's Values on the Client

Therapists, teachers, school counselors, child-study team members, lawyers, clergy, physicians, and other mental health professionals who work with divorced adults or children of divorce, not only have their own value systems regarding divorce but also are in a powerful position to communicate their values to vulnerable, and often confused, divorcing parents and children.

Family members experiencing divorce find their previously held values threatened. They cannot rely on their old values regarding the importance of the intact family or the roles of various family members. They wonder: Who is my family and who am I in relation to others? How important am I to my family members and they to me? Are people trustworthy? What does love mean? How important is it for me to remain in my house? Do I need to be both a mother and father to my child? These are but a few of the issues involving values that face the person in crisis. As clients try to answer these questions, they look to the expert with whom they are in contact. Even if they do not directly question the experts, they are unconsciusly aware of and respond to the expert's values. Quite often, therapists are told by clients that they told them something, when indeed they did not. Often, it is instead the therapist's values and attitudes that were conveyed.

Although the value systems of children are not as complex, systematized, or as well defined as that of an adult, children also experience value upheaval and undergo changes in their values. They may question their beliefs about the importance of living within an intact family, the permanence of love, the importance of marriage and relationships, etc. They may notice changes in ways in which their parents want them to relate to them and changes in how they are treated by friends or relatives. Like their parents, they consciously and unconsciously look to authority figures around them to help clarify the confusion. Again, the therapist can play a crucial role.

We recommend that mental health professionals try, not only to remain aware of value conflicts within their clients, but also to remain keenly aware of their own values. As clients search for new values that are "right," they may try to determine and incorporate their perception of the professional's values. We recommend that the mental health professional help clients redevelop their own values, considering their particular situations and circumstances. However, in this book, we do present certain exceptions where situations do not warrant minimizing the impact of the professional's values on the client. The exceptions are in areas in which the parents are endangering their children physically or emotionally, and where human lives and property need to be protected from harm and destruction. In addition, we advocate cooperation with other professionals in the best interest of the clients. Certainly, such cooperation will be with the client's knowledge and consent, and the professional's use of discretion concerning with whom they communicate and what is disclosed about one's clients.

Exploring Children's and Parent's Attitudes

Transition of Values

Children acquire most of their values by identifying with and emulating their family members. Parents within intact families impart their "intact-family values" to their children without even discussing them. For instance, a family may place a premium on family togetherness. The family goes on vacations together as well as on shopping trips and on outings. They participate together in recreational activities and entertainment. Usually, there is division of responsibility or shared responsibility between the parents. Joint decisions are made. Parents support one another, take care of one another, and may be affectionate toward one another. The parents disagree and then resolve the disagreement. They argue, then make up. There is consistency, stability, and security. The value of family togetherness is clear to the children.

Children are aware when things become very different. The parents are angry all the time. There is much tension in the home. The parents do not seem to be making up. There is no affection seen. More things are done separately. The emotional separation has begun. The parents talk about living separately. The children's world becomes insecure. Although there are many variations in the above scenario, it is rather typical of what happens when a family begins to separate. Children witness significant changes. So much seems to have changed.

Then the family divides. Who takes the children? What were they told? What did they overhear? Where will they live? How often will they see their other parent? Will there no longer be any vacations together? What about holidays and birthdays? A number of parental beliefs no longer can be applied. There is a value crisis. The children ask: "What is right now?" "Is it now okay for mom to see other men?" "Whom do I ask for a raise in my allowance?" "Who will drive me to the games?" "Don't all families have a mommy and a daddy?"

The concept of a divided family may have been seen disparagingly when the family was intact: "He has no father." "His mom has to work, now." Then, the parents separate and—"Now, we are one of *those* families!" Responsibilities are no longer shared; the custodial parent assumes all responsibility when the children are present and the noncustodial parent assumes all responsibility when the children are visiting. Children from separated families may witness their parents in conflict. They may see parental abuse—verbal or even physical. One parent may demean the other parent who was once held in high esteem. Once there was encouragement to emulate a parent, now there may be discouragement for the same actions. Children may see their parents refuse to talk to one another or refuse to discuss problems or to make joint decisions. The children may see their parents romantically linked to another adult. They may get less parental attention and may need to rely more on themselves and their siblings to get their needs met.

Resolution of the Value Crisis

What was once the expected, the "natural," and the "good"—what was once valued has undergone significant change. The value changes do not mean that children no longer consider family togetherness or an intact family environment as the ideal. They still frequently do, causing them to envy this in others or make numerous attempts to pull their parents back together. Some children try to accomplish this by manipulating.

> Daniel, age 9, openly demonstrated his distress to his parents about their separation. He openly mourned, openly fantasized his wish to have the family reunite, and frequently suggested that the other parent take part in activities planned.

> When the child realized (after 4 years and after his father's remarriage), that his previous family was lost to him, he created much conflict with his mother—to the point that his mother requested that the father take custody of him. As his conflict with his mother was explored in his therapy, and as the reasons for his actions became clearer, he said: "If I can't have my first family, at least I can try again with a second family."

Some children attempt in the therapeutic atmosphere to pair the therapists with the opposite sex parent. The manipulative attempts may be subtle, but the therapist needs to be aware of the possibility of the child making such attempts and to interpret these to the child.

In order to help resolve and come to terms with value changes, children watch and listen to how their parents cope with the changes in their lives. Does the parent seek help? Are attempts made to discuss the changes and feelings with friends or with the other parent? Does the parent drink alcohol, or get angry easily? Is there recognition from the parent that the child is experiencing similar exposure to value changes? Does the parent talk to the child and encourage the child to talk to friends, a therapist or counselor, or a teacher? Does the parent provide books about family changes for the child to read?

Resolution is not easy. Several years may be needed to reach a point of acceptance of the situation. New values, perhaps more flexible, develop. Life can still be fun and needs can still be met. Although an intact family atmosphere might still be considered "the best," in reality, things may be better now with greater independence and a calmer home atmosphere. Maybe the new step-parent is really nice. There still are many good times with both parents, although separately.

Some resolutions take longer. Sometimes a third person, an outsider, needs to talk to the parent(s) and children. For some parents and children, the value changes or differences between the values held and their lives, need to be made explicit, the losses grieved, and new values formed or the "new reality" accepted.

How can the mental health professional help parents come to terms with their value conflicts or the disparity between their present lives and their old values? Naming the values is the first step of one approach: "It appears that having your wife give a second opinion about whether you did the right thing was very important to you;" "You seem to keep trying to duplicate what you once had." The identification of values helps clarify confusion, and helps the parent realize one source of anxiety or depression. Then, they can decide how to approach the changes—choosing between continuing to try to re-capture the loss or to change some of the values.

A second approach begins with the parent's exposure to the values of others. Here, either a family therapy approach or group approach is useful. Such exposure helps parents evaluate and deter-mine whether or not other values are applicable to them in their new situation. They can pick and choose, and then apply the behaviors that go along with the values. At times, the behaviors may work for them and the accompanying values feel comfortable. For others, a trial-and-error approach is useful, with changes until comfortable new be-haviors are found.

Certainly, it is most helpful for the children if the parent is able to feel comfortable with new or modified values and behaviors before much time has passed. With consistency and stability in the parent's life, children more easily can reach a point of consistency and stability in their own lives.

Influence of Parental Values and Attitudes on Children

Just as the parents' influence is important in how well the children are able to adjust to the value changes, the parents are also crucial influ-ences in the area of attitudes. Klebanow (1976) discussed the impor-tance of how the parents view themselves and view their children. "Does the parent view himself or herself as damaged and defective as a consequence of the single state? Is the absence or loss of the other parent perceived as catastropic crippling, or as a reparable wound? . . . Has marriage been renounced? . . . Are the children viewed as burdens who interfere with the pursuit of pleasure or career, or as joyful, although trying?" (p. 42). Such parental perceptions may lead the chil-dren to view themselves differently.

Ambivalence

Separated parents have a delicate balance to maintain—taking care of themselves with sensitivity to their own needs and changes, and yet saving sufficient energy to meet the needs of their children. The sometimes burdensome responsibility of tending to the children's needs at a time when the parents have many unfulfilled needs of their own, leads some parents to have ambivalent feelings toward their children. As much as they love their children, they may feel angry, resentful, burdened, and so on.

Weiss (1979) recognized the ambivalence, for example, at times when parents resent the children for restrictions placed on them or for reminding them of a "mistaken relationship." As a result of the ambivalent feelings, the parents may reject their children, may compensate through overprotection, might foster independence before the children are ready, or, in their attempt to console themselves, they may overlook problems.

The mental health professional can help parents recognize that it is normal to have ambivalent feelings toward their children. They can help parents understand that they may be treating their children in a manner that satisfies their own needs or fears as opposed to doing what is best for their children.

Custodial Parent

The parent with custody has the responsibility of raising the children alone, often with little support or relief from the noncustodial parent. There may be guilt over placing the child with a babysitter and worry about the negative influence of the noncustodial parent. A parent wanting relief from the children may find it difficult to find because of guilt feelings.

Custodial parents, more than anyone else, provide the model for the child during this time of change. These parents, realizing their expanded importance in their children's lives, may find it difficult to balance the fulfillment of their needs with those of their children. However, looking out only for the children's needs or sacrificing and denying oneself repeatedly for the children will serve to breed anger, resentment, or even depression. As a result, parents need to be "selfish" sometimes. They need to be with other adults and to engage in activities that give them pleasure. The children, in turn, learn that it is not necessary to be worried or overly concerned about their parent at this time. They can continue to be children because the parent is taking care of himself or herself.

Some custodial parents expect the child to fulfill the roles and meet the needs that the other parent either did or did not meet. This may range from sleeping in the absent parent's bed to performing "adultlike" chores. Using the child as a "sounding board" for the parent's feelings after the separation is another way the parent may use the child to replace the absent parent. The parent may be feeling lonely, angry toward the other parent, fatigued with extra work and responsibility, and sometimes wishful that the noncustodial parent would take the children. When children repeatedly hear these feelings from a parent or repeatedly witness the nonverbal expression of the parent's unhappy feelings (such as crying a great deal or neglecting themselves), they tend to become overly involved in their homelife. Overinvolvement can leave children with lessened ability to deal with problems or situations outside of their home, and the children may develop learning difficulties or become involved in altercations with peers.

In a group for children of divorce, 11-year-old Jonathan gave advice to a new child whose parents had just separated. "Don't talk about your father in front of your mother, or she'll start to cry and you'll have to take care of her." Jonathan seemed to be handling his parents' divorce well. He could verbalize about his problems and take care of his mother when she was overwhelmed by her feelings. However, his school work was suffering because, according to him, he just couldn't concentrate. Jonathan was clearly an over-involved child whose mother needed help in dealing with her feelings. The group leader contacted the mother to suggest that she seek treatment and learned that she recently had begun to see a therapist.

Noncustodial Parent

Since the noncustodial parent sees the child less frequently, what occurs during the shortened time period together can have more impact on the child than if the same thing occurred in conjunction with many other incidents or numerous expressions of feelings.

Noncustodial parents frequently seem dissatisfied with how the children are being raised and view themselves as ineffectual in making an impact on the children in their time spent together. They may also feel reluctant to discipline the children for fear that the children will not want to see them as often or will provide negative information to the custodial parent that would interfere with visitation privileges or with the relationship they, as the other parent, have with the custodial parent. On the other hand, during the visit, they may attempt to undo what the other parent has done or do what the custodial parent has not done, making the visitation tense and unenjoyable for all.

Noncustodial parents may experience a feeling of deprivation. Perhaps they are unable to see their children as often as they would like. Perhaps they were the "losers" in a custody battle. Such feelings of deprivation, unimportance, anger, impotence, separateness, or loss might cause parents to use their children to compensate for these feelings. They may keep the children longer than the agreed upon time. They may lavish gifts upon the children. They may speak disparagingly of the other parent. The child may become a "weapon" with which the parent could demonstrate higher power, or through which revenge could be achieved.

Certainly, such feelings, especially when the child becomes the object of the feelings or is seen as the one who can be used to resolve the feelings, interfere with the parent-child relationship and create confusion in the children. The children may either try to help the parent or begin to avoid that parent.

Conclusion

This chapter has been devoted to an exploration of values and attitudes—such as how they develop, how the divorce process alters them, and how the mental health professionals should be aware of the influence of their values and attitudes on the vulnerable client.

In general, we recommend an approach that allows parents to reformulate their own values and attitudes, and reduce overdependency on the therapist. The role of the mental health professional can be to help parents recognize changes in themselves, recognize changes in their children, and develop alternate coping strategies with an emphasis on helping the children separate their lives from their parent's marital or personal problems.

Epilogue
Looking Ahead

This book was written with a two-fold purpose: (1) to familiarize the reader with the current literature and research, providing a single sourcebook for mental health professionals who work with divorcing families; and (2) to present the reader with possible applications of such knowledge to the therapeutic process. The focus is on the relationship between the mental health professional and the parents in the interest of the children. The book is not intended to provide a framework for direct intervention with children of divorce, nor does the book provide the reader with a single model of intervention for parents. It presents an overview of possible strategies (supported by the literature) useful to the mental health professional.

Research Needs

The limitations of the research are evident. There is much that we still do not know about divorced parents and their children. We need to take a closer look at joint custody, for example. Legislation has been introduced in several states that would make joint custody the presumed model. However, this has been done without research evidence of the benefits of joint custody. Furthermore, a distinction may need to be made between joint custody meaning a continuation of the legal and ethical responsibilities of both parents, and joint custody meaning shared physical custody.

We need to know more about the children who adjust satisfactorily to their parents' divorce. As mental health professionals, we have a tendency to focus on the etiology of psychopathology. However, a better understanding of the capacities and coping skills of children who do adjust well can help us develop more appropriate intervention strategies for those who do not. Similar studies of parents who cope well are vital for the same reasons. Further research into outcome of therapeutic intervention would be useful in ascertaining the appropriateness and usefulness of various intervention strategies with this particular population.

Over the years, we shall need longitudinal data to answer other questions about children of divorce. What will their expectations for marriage be like, or divorce? What will their marriage rate be? How likely will they be to use divorce as a solution to their marital problems? How likely will they be to have children?

Early Prevention

There are a number of ways to prevent the development of divorce-related psychopathology. Ideally, the most effective means would be a major reduction in the divorce rate. Perhaps by adding marriage and parenting courses to the high school curriculum, we can better prepare young people for what is involved in both, and give them realistic expectations of the work and responsiblity that accompany the pleasures.

Even after a divorce is in process, there are steps that can be taken that can lessen the likelihood of problems emerging in the children. The adversarial means of reaching custody decisions can be abandoned. Custody can be determined apart from the settlement of property, alimony, and even child-support issues. Mandatory counseling for parents becoming divorced can be tied to the granting of the final decree. In that way parents can be educated regarding the problems common to divorced parents, and helped to avoid the common pitfalls. Supportive programs for children of divorce can be made widely available for early intervention, prior to the emergence of symptoms.

In order to accomplish the goal of early prevention, mental health professionals, legislators, judges, lawyers, educators, and parents need to cooperate in bringing about the necessary changes.

Advocating the Child's Position

Children need someone to advocate their position, to offer them support, and to meet their needs when their parents are divorcing and the structure of the family is changing. Mental health professionals in schools, community mental health centers, and private practice are in a position to act as advocates for the children and to see that parents, teachers, and the courts are responding to their needs. In any setting in which they work, mental health professionals must create opportunities for the children and the significant others in their lives to learn and grow, to develop insight and skills in coping with the problems created by divorce, and ultimately, to reduce the stress created by the divorce.

The key is creativity on the part of mental health professionals in bringing service where none has existed; in reaching educators and lawyers with information about the needs of children; and in keeping divorcing parents focused on their responsibility to their children.

Appendix A

Sample Lesson from the Post-Divorce Parenting Program

Four Ways to Minimize Children's Reactions to Divorce

Goal:

Parents understand typical reactions to divorce.

Behavioral objective:

Parents learn how to keep children's negative reactions minimal.

Materials needed:

- Chalkboard or large paper and felt tip pen
- Homework Notebook
- Leader's Manual

Procedure:

Leader:

Homework Sharing (15 minutes):

Good afternoon (evening). Last week for homework you were to observe yourself as a parent, and write down an example of the way that you followed each rule of good parenting. Will someone tell us about how you were a good model? *Elicit an example of each rule.*

Lecture/Discussion (15 minutes):

Divorce is a stressful time for all involved. Sometimes, it feels less painful just to talk about it. But, visualize yourself in a situation in which someone you're very close to, such as a close friend, moves away with no explanation, perhaps without a goodbye. How confused you would be! You might even wonder what you did wrong to make that friend leave. Now consider how children feel when their parents separate and no explanation is given—how confused they must be!

Many parents assume that when children are young, and do not yet have command of the language, they can't comprehend an explanation and, therefore, don't need to be told. Sometimes, this assumption makes it easier for the parent who doesn't want to talk about the divorce. But, studies have shown that children recover better from the divorce experience when they've been told that mommy and daddy won't be living together anymore and why.

It's never too late to explain the divorce to children in simple, sincere words that they can understand. If the children were under 2 when the parents separated, no explanation was probably possible. As the child gets older, wait until he asks a question relating to the separation, then honestly answer the question. It's important to give the children the type of information that indicates that they are still loved by both parents, that the divorce decision had to do with mommy and daddy alone and had nothing to do with the children, and that they will continue to live with one parent and be visited by the other. Remember, if you haven't given your children this information yet, it's not too late. Simply explain it when the opportunity appears, such as when the situation may be different because one parent is absent, or explain when the children ask questions. Explain the divorce or separation in language appropriate to the age of the child and in a way that sensitively predicts their concerns. An example of how to explain the divorce to a child is as follows: (both parents should be present at the time, if possible)

> Mommy and daddy have decided not to live together anymore. We know we will argue less if we don't live together. You will live with mommy, and daddy will see you every Saturday and talk to you on the telephone. It's going to take time to get accustomed to this, but we can talk about it whenever you'd like.

Such an explanation provides *Way* 1 to minimize children's negative reactions to the divorce.

Are there any questions or comments? (Allow a few minutes for discussion.)

It is important for the child to continue to see the noncustodial parent. Research has shown that negative effects are less, even if the relationship is sporadic or the noncustodial parent unreliable, if the child continues to see that parent. Therefore, *Way* 2 to keep negative effects to a minimum is to help the child maintain contact with the noncustodial parent. This contact may be through visits, phone calls, letters; all should be encouraged.

Can anyone give us an example of how allowing free visitation has been helpful to your child? (Allow 1 or 2 examples.)

Way 3 to minimize the negative reactions in the child is to avoid the triangling of the child between parents. *Triangling* is the formation of an emotionally hot threesome. Even though your spouse or former spouse may anger *you*, or hurt *you*, this is between *you* and that person. Your child should not be involved. Some children become messengers for parents who are not talking. Some parents refuse visitation or don't bring the children home on time when they are angry with their former spouse. Some parents say things to the child about the other parent that they are afraid to say directly to the other parent. Even if you are not on good terms with your spouse or former spouse, remember that both of you still are parents, and need to remain objective with each other where the children are concerned.

This can be difficult to do. Have any of you ever been caught in the triangle? (Elicit a few examples.)

. *Way* 4 is to respond to changes in children's behavior which you, as a parent, suspect may be related to the divorce. If an active child becomes overly quiet, or an obedient child becomes unmanageable, or an independent child begins to cling, it may be that he or she is acting out feelings about the divorce that have not been expressed. Seize each opportunity to discuss and clarify feelings and information about the divorce.

I wonder if any of you have done this and if you could tell us how your children reacted?

I am going to divide you into groups. I will present a vignette to each group. Each vignette describes a problem of a child of a different age. The groups will follow the directions, choosing someone among you to record the responses. Then each group will share its solutions to the problem with the others, for discussion purposes.

(15 minutes): The leader will randomly divide the participants into groups. Have the group members turn to pages 4 and 5 in their Homework Notebook where the vignettes are printed. Four vignettes are provided regarding children ages 3½, 6, 11, 15. Choose three of the four vignettes that most closely approximate the age group of the children whose parents are participants in this program.

Group 1: Age 3½

A 3½-year-old child, Beth, whose parents separated a week earlier, cries, clinging to her mother's skirt when the mother tries to leave Beth with a sitter while she shops.

What do you think is going on? How do you think the mother and father should have handled the situation?

Group 2: Age 6

Joshua, a 6-year-old, whose parents have been separated for 4 months, frequently tells the father that he wishes he and mommy would live together again.

What do you think is going on? How do you think the father and mother should handle Joshua?

Group 3: Age 11

Susie, age 11, begins to play less frequently with her peers. She watches television more. The teacher calls the mother to report that Susie doesn't seem to want to play with the other children and wants to stay in the building at recess time. The parents have been separated for one week.

What do you think is going on? How can the mother and father deal with Susie's problem?

Group 4: Age 15

David's mother notices that he no longer comes to her as frequently with his problems with girls or with information about school. Up to age 15, David had always come to her with such information. The mother, separated for six months, wonders if this is related to the divorce and how to handle it?

What do you think is going on? How can the parents deal with this situation?

(30 minutes): The leader says: Would each group choose a spokesperson to present the vignette, what your group thought was going on, and your group's suggestions for handling the situation.

The groups choose a spokesperson. The leader facilitates discussion with such comments as:

Are there comments?
Who else would like to respond?
    What do the others think of their interpretations and methods of resolution?

Possible responses to the vignettes are as follows:

Group 1: 3½-year-old child

Possible Interpretation:

Child may be fearful mother will leave like daddy left and will not return.

Possible Methods to Handle:

1. Mother can leave child with familiar sitter or relative.
2. Mother should tell child where she is going (e.g., shopping) and will return by specified time (e.g., 2 P.M.). This alleviates child's confusion and anxiety. Child can "watch the clock" with the sitter. (Of course, the parent should give herself enough time to insure that returning earlier than the specified time is a certainty.)
3. The child should be assured that mommy will return as she always does and that the sitter will play with her until mommy returns.
4. Have the sitter or relative watch the child in the parent's home.
5. When daddy sees the child, it's again important to explain that because mommy and daddy don't live together, doesn't mean he won't see her anymore. (He'll still see her every Saturday at noon, for example.)

Group 2: 6-year-old child

Possible Interpretation:

Joshua may be manipulating a little to try to get his parents back together again. Or, the boy might just be expressing a wish common for children of divorce at this age level.

Possible methods to handle:

1. Daddy can tell Joshua again that mommy and daddy have made the decision not to live together.
2. Daddy can tell him that he can wish this if he wants, but wishing won't make it happen.
3. Mommy can also reiterate to Joshua when the situation warrants, about the decision to separate.

Group 3: 11-year-old child

Possible Interpretation:

It is common for children of this age to feel shame about their parent's divorce. Susie might be fearful her peers will find out, or ask her embarrassing questions.

Possible Methods to Handle:

1. The parents(s) can explore with Susie possible reasons for her isolation.
2. Parent(s) can ask her whether she has told any of her friends.
3. Parent(s) can ask whether any of her friends have divorced parents.
4. Parent(s) can tell her it's okay to talk about the divorce with her friends and that it's nothing to be ashamed of.
5. Parent(s) can provide books regarding children of divorce, and discuss them with her.

Group 4: 15-year-old boy

Possible Interpretation:

David may be going through a normal adolescent distancing from parents that may be exaggerated or have come on sooner as a result of the divorce.

Possible Methods to Handle:

1. The parent(s) can understand and allow this distancing. Often the adolescent chooses peers or a teacher with whom to talk.
2. If the problem seems to be acute, the parent(s) can ask the school counselor to speak to the child or ask the child if he wants to talk to a therapist. If he doesn't, the parents can go to one, getting help for themselves around how to help David through this.

(10 minutes): If time permits, the leader can read the one vignette not used for the groups, thus getting the entire group of parents to participate in determining possible interpretations and methods for dealing with the problem. The group leader will sum up by saying the following:

Before we leave, I think it important to sum up what we learned tonight. Could someone tell me one way to minimize a negative reaction in our children.

Leader writes the answer on the chalkboard, then elicits another response until all 4 ways are listed. A review of the 4 ways we discussed are listed below:

1. Explain the divorce to your child in sincere, age-appropriate terms.
2. Maintain the children's contact with the noncustodial parent.
3. Avoid triangling the child between parents.
4. Handle changes in children's behavior with sensitivity, realizing they may be related to the divorce.

Homework assignment (5 minutes):

Let's look at this week's homework assignment. Open to page ___ in your Notebook (see Figure A.1.). I would like you now to rate yourself in each area designated. For example, if you think you do well generally in helping your child maintain contact (or at least not discouraging contact) with the noncustodial parent, then give yourself a 1 or a 2 in the space provided.

You will rate yourself again in these areas at the beginning of next week's session. This is to provide you with a measure of your skill and your growth in these areas. You'll be able to note which areas still need your further attention.

Each day this week, place a check in the boxes for *Ways #1, 2, 3, 4* if they apply to you on that day. For example, if your child asked you a question about the divorce and you answered the question, put a check (x) under that day.

Good night. See you next week.

Figure A.1.

Parents' Rating Sheet

1 = excellent; 2 = good; 3 = average; 4 = marginal; 5 = poor

How well did you do in minimizing possible negative reactions to the divorce/separation?

	Beginning Rating (#)	Day 1 (x)	Day 2 (x)	Day 3 (x)	Day 4 (x)	Day 5 (x)	Day 6 (x)	Day 7 (x)	End-of-Week Rating (#)
Way #1 I talked to my child about the divorce									
Way #2 I did not discourage contact with the non-custodial parent									
Way #3 I did not involve my child in a triangle									
Way #4 I responded to changes in my children's behavior which might be related to the divorce									

Appendix B

Bibliography for Professionals, Parents, and Children

I. For Professionals

Arnold, L. E. (Ed.). *Helping parents help their children*. New York: Brunner/ Mazel, 1978. Collection of articles on parent guidance and parent education.

Gardner, R. A. *Psychotherapy with children of divorce*. New York: Jason Aronson, 1976. Applies Gardner's therapy techniques to this population. Includes the social, emotional, and legal aspects of divorce.

Levinger, G., & Moles, O. C. (Eds.). *Divorce and separation: Context, causes, and consequences*. New York: Basic Books, 1979.

Rosenthal, K. M., & Keshet, H. F. *Fathers without partners*. Totowa, NJ: Rowman & Littlefield, 1980. A study of fathers and the family after marital separation.

Stuart, I., & Abt, L. *Children of separation and divorce: Management and treatment*. New York: Van Nostrand Reinhold, 1981. A compendium of works regarding children of divorce in a variety of settings and conditions including medico-legal considerations, psychodynamics, management of behavior associated with marital discord, and treatment within a family unit.

Tessman, L. H. *Children of parting parents*. New York: Jason Aronson, 1978. Theoretical material and detailed case studies.

Visher, E. G., & Visher, M. O. *Stepfamilies: A guide to working with stepparents and stepchildren*. New York: Brunner/Mazel, 1979. Reviews the problems of reconstituted families and offers suggestions for overcoming them.

Wallerstein, J. S., & Kelly, J. B. *Surviving the breakup: How children and parents cope with divorce*. New York: Basic Books, 1980. A report of their five-year study of divorced families in California.

Weiss, R. *Marital separation*. New York: Basic Books, 1976. Helps professionals understand the process of divorce and its complexities.

II. For Parents

Atkin, E., & Ruben, E. *Part-time father: A guide for the divorced father*. New York: Vanguard Press, 1976. Intended to help noncustodial fathers maintain a relationship with their children.

Duncan, T. R., & Duncan, D. *You're divorced but your children aren't*. Englewood Cliffs, NJ: Prentice-Hall, Inc., 1979. Practical, simple parenting guide.

Galper, M. *Co-parenting: A source book for the separated or divorced family*. Philadelphia: Running Press, 1978.

Gardner, R. A. *The parents book about divorce*. Garden City, NY: Doubleday, 1977. Rather technical for most parents, but very comprehensive.

Hope, K., & Young, N. (Eds.). *Momma: A sourcebook for single mothers*. New York: New American Library, 1976. A compilation of articles, with practical advice for single mothers.

Roman, M., & Haddad, W. *The disposable parent: The case for joint custody*. New York: Holt, Rinehart & Winston, 1978. Strong argument for joint custody.

Turow, R. *Daddy doesn't live here anymore*. Garden City, NY: Anchor Books, 1978. A guide to help parents anticipate children's needs during the divorce process.

Weiss, R. S. *Going It Alone*. New York: Basic Books, 1979. Practical suggestions for the single parent regarding childrearing and conducting own life.

Wheeler, M. *Divided children: A legal guide for divorcing parents*. New York: W. W. Norton & Co., 1980. A guide to custody law and legal problems that parents confront during and following divorce.

III. For Children*

Pre-school children

Adams, F. *Mushy eggs*. NY: Putnam, 1973. The story of a family managing after divorce.

Berger, T. *A friend can help*. Raintree Publishers, 1974. Stresses the importance of having a friend with whom to discuss parental divorce.

Clifton, L. *Everett Anderson's friend*. NY: Holt, Reinhart & Winston, 1976. A child who thinks about how his father would have helped him.

Goff, B. *Where is daddy?* Boston: Beacon Press, 1969. Written to help preschoolers cope with grief, loneliness, and confusion after parental separation.

Kindred, W. *Lucky Wilma*. Dial Press, 1973. Presents a good relationship between a visiting father and his daughter.

*The authors wish to acknowledge the following sources used in compiling this bibliography:

Dreyer, S. S. *The bookfinder: A guide to children's literature about the needs and problems of youth aged 2–15*. Circle Pines, MN: American Guidance Service, Inc., 1977.

Journal of Clinical Child Psychology, 6 (2). Separation and divorce—selected readings for children and adolescents.

Journal of Divorce, Vol. 1–4, Book Reviews, edited by Craig A. Everett.

Lexan, J. M. *Emily and the klunky baby and the next door dog.* New York: Dial Press, 1972. Story about a child who feels neglected after her parents divorce.

Rogers, H. S. *Morris and his brave lion.* New York: McGraw-Hill, 1975. Unrealistic ending, but otherwise a good treatment of divorce.

Sinberg, J. *Divorce is a grown-up problem.* New York: Avon Books, 1978. A coloring book which helps children understand what they need to know when their parents first separate.

Thomas, I. *Eliza's Daddy.* New York: Harcourt, Brace, Jovanovich, 1976. Deals with remarriage.

Zindel, P. *I love my mother.* New York: Harper & Row, 1975. Story about a small boy living with a divorced mother.

Elementary School children

Anchor, C. *Last night I saw Andromeda.* Walch, 1975. Story about an 11-year-old girl who tries to win divorced father's love.

Bawden, N. *Runaway summer.* New York: Lippincott, 1969. An angry frustrated child of divorce tries to deal with problems by running from them.

Blue, R. *A month of Sundays.* Franklin Watts, 1972. A 10-year-old boy adjusts to his parent's separation. His parents convince him that it isn't his fault.

Blume, J. S. *It's not the end of the world.* Bradbury Press, 1972. An 11-year-old girl copes with separation and her reconciliation fantasies.

Brenenfeld, F. *Mom and dad are getting a divorce!* Minnesota: EMC Corporation, 1980. The story of a boy and girl who tell "how it is." The purpose of the book is to help children acknowledge and communicate feelings about the divorce.

Cleaver, V., & Cleaver, B. *Lady Ellen Grae.* New York: J. B. Lippincott, 1968. A intelligent 11-year-old girl lives with her father during the summer, but has to adjust to living with other relatives during the school year.

Ewing, K. *A private matter.* New York: Harcourt, Brace, Jovanovich, 1975. A girl must give up a fantasied father when her mother remarries.

Secondary School children

Arundel, H. *A family failing.* Thomas Nelson, 1972. An 18-year-old girl experiences the disintegration of her family and learns to view her parents as people apart from herself.

Barnwell, R. D. *Shadow on the water.* David McKay, 1972. A 13-year-old girl responds to the painful situation between her parents.

Bradbury, B. *The blue year.* Ives Washburn, 1967. A 17-year-old girl believes at first that she has caused her parents to divorce. She goes away to college rather than deal with her problems with her mother.

Holland, I. *Heads you win, tails I lose.* J. B. Lippincott, 1973. The story of an overweight 15-year-old whose parents battle constantly and finally separate.

Koob, T. *The deep search.* J. B. Lippincott, 1969. A story about an 11th-grade girl whose parents separate because they cannot deal with problems of raising a younger, retarded child.

Mazer, H. *Guy Lenny*. Delacorte Press, 1971. A 12-year-old boy is the focal point of a bitter custody battle.

Richards, A., & Willis, I. *How to get it together when your parents are coming apart*. Nonfiction. Presents examples of what adolescents cope with and how to cope.

Smith, D. B. *Kick a stone home*. Crowell, 1974. Although her father has remarried, a 15-year-old girl still hopes for her parents to reunite and struggles with her feelings.

Stoltz, M. S. *Leap before you look*. Harper & Row, 1972. A pubescent girl feels rejected when her father moves out and she has difficulty adjusting to his remarriage.

Gardner, R. A. *The boys and girls book about divorce*. New York: Jason Aronson, 1971. Candid discussion of many real concerns of children of divorce; with an introduction for parents.

Greene, C. *A girl called Al*. Viking, 1969. An absent father's money is no substitute for his love and the custodial mother learns to be more attentive.

Klein, N. *Taking sides*. Pantheon, 1973. A girl who lives with her divorced father is confused by the many disruptions in her life.

Lexau, J. M. *Me day*. Dial Press, 1971. Presents the events leading to a divorce. The parents both care about the children and do not try to force the boys into an alliance.

Lisker, S. *Two special cards*. Harcourt, Brace, Jovanovich, 1976. Realistic portrayal of a visiting father and custodial mother.

Mona, P. *My Dad lives in a downtown hotel*. Doubleday, 1973. A boy feels he is to blame for his parents' divorce and is ashamed to tell anyone.

Mozer, N. *I, Tressy*. Delacorte, 1971. The story of a girl's angry feelings about her parents' divorce.

Newfield, M. *A book for Jodan*. Atheneum, 1975. A 9-year-old girl doubts that her parents still love her after their separation.

Norris, G. *Lillian*. Atheneum, 1968. Shows the insecurity a girl feels after her parents separate and her struggle to become self-reliant.

Platt, K. *Chloris and the creeps*. Chilton Book Co., 1973. All men that Chloris' divorced mother dates are unacceptable to her.

Walitzer, H. *Out of love*. Farrar, Straus & Giroux, Inc., 1976. A girl schemes to reunite her parents.

References

Abidin, R. *Parenting skills: Trainer's manual.* New York: Human Sciences Press, 1975.

Adam, K. S., Lohrenz, J. G., & Harper, D. Suicidal ideation and parental loss. *Canadian Psychiatric Association Journal,* 1973, *18,* (2), 95–99.

Ahrons, C. R. Joint custody arrangements in post-divorce families. *Journal of Divorce,* 1980, *3,* (3), 189–205.

Ahrons, C. R. The continuing coparental relationship between divorced spouses. *American Journal of Orthopsychiatry,* 1981, *51,* (3), 415–428.

Alexander, S. J. Influential factors on divorced parents in determining visitation arrangements. *Journal of Divorce,* 1980, *3,* (3), 223–240.

Arnold, L. E. Parents' groups. In L. E. Arnold (Ed.), *Helping parents help their children.* New York: Brunner/Mazel, 1978.

Arnold, L. E. Strategies and tactics of parent guidance. In L. E. Arnold (Ed.), *Helping parents help their children.* New York: Brunner/Mazel, 1978.

Bower, E. M. Primary prevention in school setting. In G. Caplan (Ed.), *Prevention of mental disorders in children.* New York: Basic Books, 1961.

Bureau of the Census. *Divorce, child custody, and child support.* Washington, D.C.: U.S. Government Printing Office, 1979.

Calvin, D. A. Joint custody: As family and social policy. In I. R. Stuart and L. E. Abt, (Eds.), *Children of separation and divorce: Management and treatment.* New York: Van Nostrand Reinhold, 1981.

Cantor, D. W. *Evaluation of a parenting skills training program with the parents of 1st grade children at-risk.* Unpublished doctoral dissertation, 1976.

Cantor, D. W. Model initiated in school: groups for children of divorce. In W. Pryzwansky (Chair), *Collaboration between health center and school psychological services.* Symposium presented to meeting of American Psychological Association, Toronto, August 1978.

Cantor, D. W. School-based groups for children of divorce. *Journal of Divorce,* 1977, *1,* (2), 183–187.

Chiriboga, D. A., Coho, A., Stein, J. A., & Roberts, J. Divorce, stress and social supports: A study of help-seeking behavior. *Journal of Divorce,* 1979, *3,* (2), 121–135.

Coche, J., & Goldman, J. Brief psychotherapy for women after divorce: Planning a focused experience. *Journal of Divorce,* 1979, *3,* (2), 153–160.

Cowen, E. L., Trost, M. A., Izzo, L. D., Lorion, R. P., Dorr, D., & Isaacson, R. V. *New ways in school mental health.* New York: Human Sciences Press, 1975.

Derdeyn, A. P. A consideration of legal issues in child custody contests. *Archives of General Psychiatry,* 1976, *33,* 165–171. (a)

Derdeyn, A. P. Child custody contests in historical perspective. *American Journal of Psychiatry*, 1976, *133*, (12), 1369–1375. (b)

Divorce: Its impact on children and youth. *Journal of Clinical Child Psychology*, Summer 1977, *6*, (2).

Drake, E. A. The role of the educator-clinician. In W. B. Pryzwansky (Chair), *Collaboration between community mental health center and school psychological services*. Symposium presented to the American Psychological Association, Toronto, 1978.

Drake, E. A. Helping the school cope with children of divorce. *Journal of Divorce*, 1979, *3*, (1), 69–75.

Drake, E. A. Children of separation and divorce: Role of the schools. In I. R. Stuart and L. E. Abt (Eds.), *Children of separation and divorce: Management and treatment*. New York: Van Nostrand Reinhold, 1981. (a)

Drake, E. A. Children of separation and divorce: School administrative policies, procedures and problems. *Phi Delta Kappan*, September 1981, 27–28. (b)

Drake, E. A. & Bardon, J. I. Confidentiality and interagency communication: effect of the Buckley Amendment. *Hospital and Community Psychiatry*, 1978, *29*, (5), 312–315.

Dullea, G. Is joint custody good for children? *New York Times Magazine*, February 3, 1980, 32–46.

Elkin, M. Post divorce counseling in a conciliation court. *Journal of Divorce*, 1977, *1*, (1), 55–65.

Felner, R. D., Stolberg, A., & Cowen, E. L. Crisis events and school mental health patterns of young children. *Journal of Consulting and Clinical Psychology*, 1975, *41*, (3), 305–310.

Fine, M. J. The parent education movement: An introduction. In M. J. Fine (Ed.), *Handbook on parent education*. New York: Academic Press, 1980.

Fulton, J. A. Parental report of children's post-divorce adjustment. *Journal of Social Issues*, 1979, *35*, (4), 126–139.

Galper, M. Co-parenting. Philadelphia: Running Press, 1978.

Gardner, R. A. *Boys and girls book about divorce*. New York: Jason Aronson, 1970.

Gardner, R. A. *Psychotherapy with children of divorce*. New York: Jason Aronson, 1976.

Gardner, R. A. *The parents book about divorce*. Garden City, N.Y.: Doubleday, 1977.

Gardner, R. A. Guidance for separated and divorced parents. In L. E. Arnold (Ed.), *Helping parents help their children*. New York: Brunner/Mazel, 1978. (a)

Gardner, R. A. Social, legal, and therapeutic changes that should lessen the traumatic effects of divorce on children. *Journal of the American Academy of Psychoanalysis*, 1978, *6* (2), 231–247. (b)

Gersick, K. G. Fathers by choice: Divorced men who receive custody of their children. In G. Levinger & O. C. Moles (Eds.), *Divorce and separation*. New York: Basic Books, 1979.

Gildea, M. D. L., Glidewell, J. C., & Kantor, N. B. The St. Louis school mental health project: History and evaluation. In E. L. Cowen, E. A. Gardner, and M. Zax (Eds.), *Emergent approaches to mental health problems*. New York: Appleton-Century-Crofts, 1967.

Glick, P. C. Children of divorced parents in demographic perspective. *Journal of Social Issues*, 1979, *35*, (4), 170–182.

Glick, P. C. & Norton, A. J. *Marrying, divorcing, and living together in the U.S. today.* Population Reference Bureau, 1977, 32, (5).

Goldman, J., & Coane, J. Family therapy after the divorce: Developing a strategy. *Family Process*, 1977, *16*, (3), 357–362.

Goldstein, J., Freud, A., & Solnit, A. J. *Beyond the best interests of the child.* New York: The Free Press, 1973.

Gordon, S. B. *The responsive parenting class: A behavioral approach to working with parents in a community mental health center.* Paper presented at the meeting of the New Jersey Psychological Association, Somerset, NJ, May 1975.

Gordon, T. *Parent effectiveness training.* New York: Wyden, 1971.

Granvold, D. K., & Welch, G. J. Intervention for post-divorce adjustment problems: The treatment seminar. *Journal of Divorce*, 1977, *1*, (1), 81–92.

Gross, R., Dibbell, J. F., & Petti, M. Family composition of students referred to child study teams. *School Psychology in New Jersey*, 1977, *19*, (1), 13–14.

Grote, D. F., & Weinstein, J. P. Joint custody: A viable and ideal alternative. *Journal of Divorce*, 1977, *1*, (1), 43–53.

Guerney, B., Jr. Filial therapy: Description and rationale. *Journal of Consulting Psychology*, 1964, *28*, (4), 304–310.

Hajal, F., & Rosenberg, E. Working with the one-parent family in family therapy. *Journal of Divorce*, 1978, *1*, (3), 259–269.

Hawkins, R. P. Universal parenthood training; a proposal for preventive mental health. In L. K. Daniels (Ed.), *The management of childhood behavior problems in school and at home.* Springfield, IL: Charles C. Thomas, 1974.

Henszey, B. N. Visitation by a non-custodial parents: What is the "best interest" doctrine? *Journal of Family Law*, 1976–77, *15*, 213–233.

Hereford, C. F. *Changing parental attitudes through group discussion.* Austin: University of Texas Press, 1963.

Hess, R. D., & Camara, K. A. Post-divorce family relationships as mediating factors in the consequences of divorce for children. *Journal of Social Issues*, 1979, *35*, (4), 79–96.

Hetherington, E. M. Effects of father absence on personality development of adolescent girls. *Developmental Psychology*, 1972, *1*, (3), 313–326.

Hetherington, E. M. Divorce: A child's perspective. *American Psychologist*, 1979, *34*, (10), 851–858.

Hetherington, E. M., Cox, M., & Cox, R. Divorced fathers. *Psychology Today*, 1977, 42–46. (a)

Hetherington, E. M., Cox, M., & Cox, R. The aftermath of divorce. In J. H. Stevens, Jr., & M. Mathews (Eds.), *Mother-Child, Father-Child Relations.* Washington, DC: NAEYC, 1977. (b)

Hodges, W. F., Wechsler, R. C., & Ballantine, C. Divorce and the pre-school child: Cumulative stress. *Journal of Divorce*, 1979, *3*, (1), 55–68.

Jacobson, D. The impact of marital separation/divorce on children: Interparent hostility and child adjustment. *Journal of Divorce*, 1978, *2*, (1), 3–19. (a)

Jacobson, D. The impact of marital separation/divorce on children: Parent-child communication and child adjustment, and regression analysis of findings from overall study. *Journal of Divorce*, 1978, *2*, (2), 175–194. (b)

Jacobson, D. The impact of marital separation/divorce on children: Parent-child separation and child adjustment. *Journal of Divorce*, 1978, *1*, (4), 341–360. (c)

Jones, S. M. Divorce and remarriage: A new beginning, a new set of problems. *Journal of Divorce*, 1978, *2*, (2), 217–227.

Kalter, N. Children of divorce in an outpatient psychiatric population. *American Journal of Orthopsychiatry*, 1977, *47*, 40–51.

Kaplan, S. L. Structural family therapy for children of divorce: Case reports. *Family Process*, 1977, *16*, (1), 75–83.

Kelly, J. B. & Wallerstein, J. S. The effects of parental divorce: Effects on the child in early latency. *American Journal of Orthopsychiatry*, 1976, *46*, (1), 20–32.

Kelly, J. B., & Wallerstein, J. S. Brief interventions with children in divorcing families. *American Journal of Orthopsychiatry*, 1977, *47*, (1), 23–36.

Keshet, H. F., & Rosenthal, K. M. The effects of different custody arrangements on the lifestyle of divorced men and their children. Paper presented at Symposium: *Children and Divorce*, Wheelock College, Boston, 1978.

Kessler, S. Building skills in divorce adjustment groups. *Journal of Divorce*, 1978, *2*, (2), 209–216.

Klebanow, S. Parenting in the single parent family. *Journal of the American Academy of Psychoanalysis*, 1976, *4*, (1), 37–48.

Kressel, K., Lopez-Morellas, M., Weinglass, J., & Deutch, M. Professional intervention in divorce: The views of lawyers, psychotherapists and clergy. In G. Levinger & O. C. Moles (Eds.), *Divorce and separation*. New York: Basic Books, 1979.

Kurdek, L. A. An integrative perspective on children's divorce adjustment. *American Psychologist*, 1981, *36*, (8) 856–866.

Kurdek, L. A., Blisk, D., & Siesky, A. E. Correlates of children's long-term adjustment to their parents' divorce. *Developmental Psychology*, 1981, *17*, (5), 565–579.

Kurdek, L. A., & Siesky, A. E. Children's perceptions of their parents' divorce. *Journal of Divorce*, 1980, *3*, (4), 339–378.

Kushner, S. The divorce, noncustodial parent and family treatment. *Social Work*, 1965, *10*, 52–58.

Lamb, M. E. The role of the father: An overview. In M. E. Lamb (Ed.), *The role of the father and child development*. New York: John Wiley & Sons, 1976.

Lamb, M. E. The effects of divorce on children's personality development. *Journal of Divorce*, 1977, *1*, (2), 163–174.

Lamb, M. E. Paternal influences and the father's role. *American Psychologist*, 1979, *34*, (10), 938–943.

Lewis, Helen B. *Psychic war in men and women*. New York: New York University Press, 1976.

Longfellow, C. Divorce in context: Its impact on children. In G. Levinger & O. C. Moles (Eds.), *Divorce and Separation*. New York: Basic Books, 1979.

Lowenstein, J. S. & Koopman, E. J. A comparison of the self-esteem between boys living with single-parent mothers and single-parent fathers. *Journal of Divorce.* 1978, *2*, (2), 195–208.

Lowery, C. R. Child custody decisions in divorce proceedings: A survey of judges. *Professional Psychology*, 1981, *12*, (4), 492–498.

Maricopa County Bar Association. *Domestic Relations Handbook*, Maricopa County Superior Court, Arizona, 1980.

McDermott, J. F. Divorce and its psychiatric sequelae in children. *Archives of General Psychiatry*, 1968, *23*, 421–427.

McGuire, J. M. Confidentiality and the child in psychotherapy. *Professional Psychology*, 1974, *5*, (4), 374–379.

Messenger, C. B., & McGuire, J. M. The child's conception of confidentiality in the therapeutic relationship. *Psychotherapy: Theory, research and practice*, 1981, *18*, (1), 123–130.

Messinger, L., & Walker, K. N. From marriage breakdown to remarriage: Parental tasks and therapeutic guidelines. *American Journal of Orthopsychiatry*, 1981, *51*, (3), 429–437.

Molinoff, D. Life with father. *New York Times Magazine*, May 22, 1977, 12–17.

Nichols, W. F. Divorce and remarriage education. *Journal of Divorce*, 1977, *1*, (2), 153–161.

Pais, J., & White, P. Family redefinition: A review of the literature toward a model of divorce adjustment. *Journal of Divorce*, 1979, *2*, (3), 271–281.

Parks, A. Children and youth of divorce in Parents Without Partners. *Journal of Clinical Child Psychology*, 1977, *6*, (2), 44–48.

Peterson, M. T. Beck vs. Beck: A more reasoned judicial response than "Kramer vs. Kramer." *New Jersey Law Journal*, September 24, 1981; 1; 18.

Pryzwansky, W., & Hodges, W. G. Effects of divorce on children: A review of empirical research. In W. F. Hodges (Chair), *Minimizing the impact of divorce on children: Two intervention approaches.* Symposium presented to the American Psychological Association, Los Angeles, 1981.

Reinhard, D. W. The reaction of adolescent boys and girls to the divorce of their parents. *Journal of Clinical Child Psychology*, 1977, *6*, (2), 21–24.

Richards, A., & Willis, I. *How to get it together when your parents are coming apart.* New York: Bantam Books, 1976.

Robb, C. Divorce Resource and Mediation Center. *New England Magazine*, *Boston Globe*, April 25, 1979.

Roman, N., & Haddad, W. *The disposable parent.* New York: Holt, Rinehart & Winston, 1978.

Rosen, R. Some crucial issues concerning children of divorce. *Journal of Divorce*, 1979, *3*, (1), 19–26.

Rowe, C. J. *An outline of psychiatry* (7th edition). Dubuque, Iowa: Wm. C. Brown, 1975.

Rozhon, T. A divorce ceremony, for children's sake. *New York Times*, August 15, 1980.

Salk, L. On the custody rights of fathers in divorce. *Journal of Clinical Psychology*, 1977, *6*, (2), 49–50.

Santrock, J. W. & Warshak, R. A. Father custody and social development in boys and girls. *Journal of Social Issues*, 1979, *35*, (4), 112–125.

Schuman, D. C. Psychiatric aspects of custody loss. In I. R. Stuart and L. E. Abt (Eds.), *Children of separation and divorce: Management and treatment.* New York: Van Nostrand Reinhold, 1981.

Schwartz, W. D. Situation/Transition groups: A conceptualization and review. *American Journal of Orthopsychiatry,* 1975, *45,* (5), 744–755.

Schwitzgebel, R. L. & Schwitzgebel, R. K. *Law and Psychological practice.* New York: John Wiley & Sons, 1980.

Seagull, A. A., & Seagull, E. The non-custodial father's relationship to his children: Conflicts and solutions. *Journal of Clinical Child Psychology,* 1977, *6,* (2) 7–11.

Sinberg, J. *Divorce is a grown-up problem.* New York: Avon Books, 1978.

Sorosky, A. D. The psychological effects of divorce on adolescents. *Adolescence,* 1977, *8,* (45), 123–136.

Spanier, G. B., & Glick, P. C. Paths to remarriage. *Journal of Divorce,* 1980, *3,* (3) 283–297.

Steinham, S. The experience of children in a joint-custody arrangement: Report of a study. *American Journal of Orthopsychiatry,* 1981, *51,* (3), 403–414.

Stryker, S. Symbolic interaction theory: A review and some suggestions for comparative research. *Journal of Comparative Family Studies,* 1972, *3,* 17–32.

Sugar, M. Children of divorce. *Pediatrics,* 1970, *46,* 588–595.

Superior Court of New Jersey: *Mayer vs. Mayer,* 1977.

Taibbi, R. Transitional relationships after divorce. *Journal of Divorce,* 1979, *2,* (3), 263–269.

Tessman, L. H. *Children of parting parents.* New York: Jason Aronson, 1978. (a)

Tessman, L. H. Working with children of parting parents: Themes and variations in adolescents. Paper presented at Symposium: *Children and Divorce,* Wheelock College, Boston, 1978. (b)

Thies, J. M. Beyond divorce: The impact of remarriage on children. *Journal of Clinical Child Psychology,* 1977, *6,* (2), 59–61.

Visher, E. B., & Visher, J. S. *Stepfamilies.* New York: Brunner/Mazel, 1979.

Wallerstein, J. S., & Kelly, J. B. The effects of parental divorce: The adolescent experience. In E. Anthony and C. Koupernick (Eds.), *The child in his family: Children at psychiatric risk* (Vol. 3). New York: John Wiley & Sons, 1974.

Wallerstein, J. S., & Kelly, J. B. The effects of parental divorce: Experiences of the pre-school child. *Journal of the American Academy of Child Psychiatry,* 1975, *14,* (4), 600–616.

Wallerstein, J. S. & Kelly, J. B. The effects of parental divorce: experiences of the child of later latency. *American Journal of Orthopsychiatry,* 1976, *46,* (2), 256–269.

Wallerstein, J. S., & Kelly, J. B. Divorce counseling: A community service for families in the midst of divorce. *American Journal of Orthopsychiatry,* 1977, *47,* (1), 4–22.

Wallerstein, J. S., & Kelly, J. B. *Surviving the breakup.* New York: Basic Books, 1980.

Warner, N. S., & Elliot, C. J. Problems of the interpretive phase of divorce-custody evaluations. *Journal of Divorce,* 1979, *2,* (4), 371–378.

Weingarten, H. & Kulka, R. Parental divorce in childhood and adult adjustment: a two generational view. In T. C. Antonucci (Chair), *Stages and crises in family life development.* Symposium presented at the meeting of the American Psychological Association, New York, September 1979.

Weiss, R. S. *Marital separation.* New York: Basic Books, 1975.

Weiss, R. S. *Going it alone.* New York: Basic Books, 1979 (a)

Weiss, R. S. Growing up a little faster: The experience of children in single parent households. *Journal of Social Issues,* 1979, *35,* (4), 97–111. (b)

Weiss, R. S. Issues in the adjudication of custody when parents separate. In G. Levinger and O. C. Moles (Eds.), *Divorce and separation.* New York: Basic Books, 1979. (c)

Whiteside, M. A., & Auerbach, L. S. Can the daughter of my father's new wife be my sister? Families of remarriage in family therapy. *Journal of Divorce,* 1978, *1,* (3), 271–283.

Worell, J. Sex-role components of maternal stress and children's well being following divorce. In S. Sobel (Chair), *The clinical psychology of women.* Symposium presented to the American Psychological Association, Los Angeles, August 1981.

Index